Buying a Business to Secure Your Financial Freedom

Finding and Evaluating the Business
That's Right for You

Ed Pendarvis, CBI
Chairman-Founder
Sunbelt Business Brokers Network

McGraw-Hill

New York   Chicago   San Francisco   Lisbon   London
Madrid   Mexico City   Milan   New Delhi   San Juan
Seoul   Singapore   Sydney   Toronto

The McGraw·Hill Companies

1 2 3 4 5 6 7 8 9 0   DOC/DOC   0 9 8 7 6 5 4

ISBN 0-07-145086-6

This publication is designed to provide accurate and authoritative information in regard to the subject matter covered. It is sold with the understanding that neither the author nor the publisher is engaged in rendering legal, accounting, futures/securities trading, or other professional service. If legal advice or other expert assistance is required, the services of a competent professional person should be sought.

> —From a declaration of principles jointly adopted by a Committee
> of the American Bar Association and a Committee of Publishers.

McGraw-Hill books are available at special quantity discounts to use as premiums and sales promotions, or for use in corporate training programs. For more information, please write to the Director of Special Sales, Professional Publishing, McGraw-Hill, Two Penn Plaza, New York, NY 10121-2298. Or contact your local bookstore.

 This book is printed on recycled, acid-free paper containing a minimum of 50% recycled, de-inked fiber.

Library of Congress Cataloging-in-Publication Data

Pendarvis, Ed.
    Buying a business to secure your financial freedom : finding and evaluating the business that's right for you / by Ed Pendarvis.
        p. cm.
    Includes index.
    ISBN 0-07-145086-6 (hardcover : alk. paper)
    1. Small business—Management. 2. Business brokerage. I. Title.
HD2341.P395   2005
658.1'62—dc22
                                      2004023704

This book is dedicated to . . .

Elaine, my wonderful wife and partner in life, who took a chance on me, and whose warm and beautiful smile always lifts my heart.

My five wonderful girls: Stephanie Myrick-Pendarvis McDonald, Elizabeth Myrick-Pendarvis Martin, Sara Pendarvis Bazemore, Melany West Warfuel, and Jennifer West Campbell. As I have tried to make a living, they have made my life worth living. I am truly a blessed man.

Every Sunbelt office owner who had the courage to join us in this adventure of private business.

The wonderful and talented folks who have added so greatly to this project. Especially to my dear friends Tom and Barbara West, who guided me through this business and this book; Elizabeth Lutyens, who translated my scribblings into English; Sue West Levine, who transformed the manuscript; and most especially Alison Van Horn, my dear friend and translator whose amazing patience and helpful suggestions were incredibly invaluable. And to the wonderful and professional folks at McGraw-Hill, especially Melissa Scuereb and Jane Palmieri, who helped bring this project to reality.

Thank you, thank you, thank you!

Contents

Contents

Preface

BEHOLD, I SHOW YOU A MYSTERY: *Buying a Business to Secure Your Financial Freedom* is about YOU, about how you choose to live your life and how you choose to provide for yourself and your family.

It might at first seem to be a book about me and my business; however, my business is trying to help folks make the right decision about how they will earn their living. Basically, you can work for someone else in a job or you can work for yourself in your own business. Both have rewards and both have risk.

With 8 million unemployed people chasing 3.5 million jobs, plus untold millions who do not like their current job, plus those who are "underemployed," consider this: provide your own job and your own job security—go into business *for* yourself, but not *by* yourself.

You can do that by buying an existing business with the present owner's help—one that has a proven track record of success, with trained employees, an existing customer base, and an immediate cash flow—or you could buy a franchise in a specific industry, with a proven track record of success and the franchisor's help.

I will show you how to do this, how to weigh the options for you and your family, and, in the process, how to purchase a business and protect yourself as best you can. There are no guarantees; but then, working for someone else is no guarantee either. There is no substitute for common sense, good self-appraisal, due diligence, and human intuition. In business as in life, you need to use all of the resources that the good Lord has provided to you.

Probably the most important decision you will make in your life is who you are going to marry. I'll leave that one to you. Next in importance is how to provide for your family and derive an income sufficient to pay for a house or apartment, a car, food, and to cover the cost of education for your children.

I can show you how to invest $40,000 to $80,000 and make at least $40,000 to $80,000 per year for the rest of your work life, that is, a 100 percent return on your money every year. Where else can you potentially get a 100 percent return on your money and have the business pay for itself?

In the United States we are free to choose our destiny, our work path, where, how, and for whom we will work for. I say, work for the man or woman you look at in the mirror. He or she truly, truly has your best interest at heart and will not let you down or fire you in midcareer.

If you manage your business well and make the necessary investment of time, money, and adjustments—or "course corrections"—to provide a product and/or a service that the marketplace responds favorably to, you just may have a job for life. Also, you have the possibility of adding great value to the business and having something to sell later on.

There has never been a better opportunity to go into business for yourself. Now is the time; where you live, or where you want to live, is the place. In *Buying a Business to Secure Your Financial Freedom*, I will show you how. I invite you to take the table of contents and, using the same or similar chapter titles, write YOUR book. The next day, the next year, the next 20 years are up to you.

Thank you for taking the time to read this book on my thoughts and advice on the real world of small business. My greatest hope is that you will find it beneficial in making some business decisions and personal decisions that will significantly help you and your family.

Best wishes and respect . . .

ED PENDARVIS, CBI
CHAIRMAN-FOUNDER
SUNBELT BUSINESS BROKERS NETWORK

1

Believing in the Value of Small Business

UNCERTAIN ECONOMIC TIMES! Job security is gone; the stock market is a roller coaster; interest on savings accounts barely keeps up with inflation; you can't live on Social Security. Where do you invest for the short term, and where do you invest for the long haul?

I say, "Invest in a sure thing—invest in yourself!"

Go into business for yourself and provide for your own job security, income, and retirement. These important accomplishments are all within your reach.

1. *Job security.* You own your own business and therefore you have a job for life. You are not subject to being laid off or downsized in midcareer through no fault of your own.

2. *Income potential.* When you take a salaried job for a certain amount of money, that is what you will make, no matter how hard or how smart you work. When you work for yourself, you have no guarantees; however, you also have no limits on your income. You may be able to make more money.

Consider the fact that a majority of big businesses started off as small businesses.

3. *Retirement program.* As you build and grow your business, you are building and growing a valuable asset that you should be able to sell when you wish to retire, and the sale of your business could produce your retirement program. You may also be able to provide jobs for others, such as your children or other family members. Compare this situation to that of a salaried employee. Employees cannot "sell" their jobs.

When you stop to think about it, what do you need out of a job or a business? You need to earn a living; an income to provide for yourself and your family. I have no doubt that the best way to accomplish and perhaps even surpass that goal is to own your own business. I will devote the next few chapters to pleading my case for that proposition. You will be the judge and jury, and I'll ask you, as a lawyer in the courtroom would, to keep an open mind until you have heard and weighed all the evidence.

This book is based on facts, feelings, experiences, and information that I have garnered and absorbed as a student of business and as a teacher of business brokerage to thousands of new business brokers and seminar attendees over the last 20 years.

One of the things I find fascinating about education is that you can give away all of your knowledge thousands of times, and you will still have just as much as when you started. Actually, you have more, because you always learn from your students. Most of my assumptions are based on life experiences, good and bad; on business experiences, successful and unsuccessful; and on my study of the real world of other businesses and business owners. I find their life stories and business stories fascinating as well as encouraging.

All successful people also have had many failures. In fact, I believe that we probably learn more from our failures than from our successes. And by the way, if you have never failed at anything—stick around. Life has a way of leveling the playing field for all of us, and that usually means some successes and some not so successes. The latter circumstance gives us opportunities to make "course corrections" as we go through life, and especially business life. In my experience, business life is a continuous stream of "course corrections."

I am a rather simple man, and I will use simple explanations and examples to present my theories on business and to convey the real value of a business to you as an individual, a family member, and a community constituent. You will find, however simple, that my "rules" do apply, and as in most games—football, for one—it's the basic, everyday blocking and tackling that ultimately help you to succeed or win.

Having had the pleasure and challenge of founding and developing the world's largest business brokerage franchise—along with some wonderful partners—I have seen some interesting business transactions as well as some interesting sellers and buyers. At Sunbelt, with over 1,500 active brokers in 300-plus locations in the United States and 11 foreign countries, we have over 10,000 businesses listed for sale and deal with over 250,000 potential buyers per year.

Since 1982, I have personally sold or helped manage the sale of over 1,000 small businesses. Now, the Sunbelt network as a whole sells over 1,000 businesses every three or four months. Each business transaction has a very important seller and a very important buyer who are trying to accomplish some very important objectives for themselves and their families. All of them want to do the best possible job to accomplish their goals through the sale and/or purchase.

To use the football metaphor again, you will find that most business sales progress three yards, two yards, five more yards, and then a first down. Then four yards, three yards, four more yards, and another first down. There are very few 99-yard runs or "Hail Mary" passes in the real world of business broker-age. However, when we get the buyer to his or her goal line, we also just got the seller to his or her goal line, and guess what? It is the very same goal line, and all teams win. Buying and selling a business should not be an adversarial transaction.

A business deal has to work for the buyer, or he or she will not buy. Likewise, it has to work for the seller, or he will not sell. It truly has to be a win-win situation or the transac-tion will not close. Furthermore, when I get the buyer and seller to their goal line, I've also managed to get myself—the business broker—to my own goal line. So it actually is a win-win-win situation!

Real-World Information

You will not find the information in this book in self-help manuals, business schools, university curricula, and certainly not at the Small Business Administration. Amazingly, even the SBA knows little about the "real world" of small business. It is perplexing to me that 98 percent of businesses in America are small business, yet all of our government and educational programs are focused on and geared toward preparing stu-dents for getting a job with or managing a big business.

We have educated five generations of Americans to get jobs with big business, but over the last 10 years the job market has shrunk, and it continues to do so. Big business has laid off hundreds of thousands of people through reengineering, downsizing, rightsizing, and offshoring, and most job growth in recent years has been in small business. Although many fine colleges and universities have initiated programs and curricula built around entrepreneurship and are doing a great job teaching the basics, most topics you would find in school still deal only with big business rules. Since big and small business are two entirely different animals, I'll go into some of the critical differences and how they affect you when it comes to earning a living, information that has been garnered over a lifetime of observing the dealings of small businesses.

The programs you find in colleges also focus on "business plans" and "start-ups," which have a difficult time in the marketplace. Some of the advantages of buying an existing business are the same as those of buying an existing house. Just as buying a house that is already functioning is usually easier and safer than building a house from scratch, deciding to "buy and build" an existing successful business or franchise is normally easier and safer than starting a business from scratch.

In fact, you will need to look at the real world of small business ownership and to understand small business value from a street-smart perspective. Armed and fortified with this information, you will be a more educated and knowledgeable buyer and/or seller. I have always found that the more educated and knowledgeable my clients and customers are, the better chance I have of helping them get to their goal line.

The Ingredients for Success

As a self-proclaimed simple man, I like to break things down into basic examples and formulas, to build a solid foundation from which both the buyer and seller can take the all-important leap of faith. Buying and/or selling a business *is* a leap of faith for both parties. There are no solid guarantees in business, just as there are no solid guarantees in life: in marriage, in having and raising children, in sports, in investments, in health, in taking a job or buying a business.

To make an educated decision, you gather your best information, seek the best professional advice, do all the necessary and available due diligence, say a prayer, or lots of prayers. Then you make the best decision you can, take a deep breath and step out onto that precipice. Take the leap: you may accomplish your basic goals of earning a living, and you just might be successful beyond your wildest dreams.

However it turns out, you are choosing a path walked before you by virtually every successful businessman or businesswoman, from Henry Ford, George Eastman, John Deere, Ray Kroc, Colonel Harland Sanders, Dave Thomas, Sam Walton, Ted Turner, and Michael Dell to Bill Gates, Oprah Winfrey, and Martha Stewart (before the stock sale). They all began with a small business and something they believed in, and through hard work, more hard work, and constant course corrections (and perhaps some divine intervention and a little luck) they built businesses that produce products and/or services that the marketplace responds to. So can you.

These winners all had two things in common:

1. They liked what they were doing.
2. They owned their own businesses.

It is nearly impossible to be very successful in business if these two ingredients are not present.

Have you ever seen or heard of a successful athlete who did not like the sport he or she was playing? A successful actor or singer who didn't like being an actor or a singer? Or a successful doctor, lawyer, or businessperson who did not like their profession? Do you think they became successful and *then* liked what they were doing, or the other way around?

If you line up what you like to do with what makes you money, you just might hit a home run. At the very least, you'll enjoy your work. It's still work, it's not play, but *liking* it gives you a much better chance of putting that extra something into your business that will make it hugely successful.

A stand-up comic on the college campus circuit in the early 1960s by the name of Brother Dave Garner used to offer this funny little line: "Don't tell me none of your doubts, man, I've got enough doubts of my own. Tell me something you believe in."

Something to Believe In

Well, I believe in the value of small business to you and to America, today more than ever. I believe that small business is the best way to provide a living for you and your family and also to provide you with job security. I believe that owning your own business offers you far and away the best opportunity to become a millionaire if you wish to. No other investment opportunity comes close. I believe that small business has provided virtually all of the job growth in the United States over the last decade.

I also believe that small business owners are the true American heroes because they make our communities, and therefore our country, work. They own and operate the local businesses that provide the goods and services that add to the richness of our life every day.

These owners get up each morning, usually before sunrise, go to work and open the local dry cleaners, restaurants, retail stores, auto repair shops, convenience stores, drugstores, coin laundries, small manufacturing companies, distributors, and local bars where, like Cheers, "everybody knows your name." They are doctors, lawyers, preachers, real estate insurance and business brokers, consultants, and owners of beauty shops. They provide jobs for anywhere from one to twenty other folks, and they meet payroll every Friday. They take care of their families, and they add significant value to our lives by making our communities work. They are on every side of the road (and every side road), and there are approximately 24 million of them.

These business owners support their families, schools, churches, and government by means of their own businesses. They are our neighbors; they're always there. You see them every day. You can count on them, and in return, they can count on you as a customer and perhaps as a friend.

CNN took a poll in 2000 asking, "Who do you trust the most?" Not surprisingly, the government and big business scored only 4 percent each on the "Trust Meter" (and this was before the Enron and WorldCom disasters). The Supreme Court ranked the highest with 44 percent; however, running a close second at 33 percent was small business. They are our neighbors, we know them and they know us. We trust each other.

Small business is "America's Amazing Economic Engine," and I'll show you how it can work for you. I'll also show you how to look at its real value and how to go about finding the right business for you and your family. We'll also cover how to buy a business at the right price, on terms and conditions that work for you, and how to protect your best interests in the process.

I hope you will find this book beneficial in building a solid foundation from which you take your "leap of faith," and, if you allow me to mix my metaphors, gain a slice of the "American pie" for yourself. It just may provide you and your family nourishment for today, for tomorrow, and for many generations to come. When you own your own business, you are investing your time and money in a sure thing: you are investing in *yourself!*

2

Some Thoughts on Going into Business for Yourself

I BELIEVE THAT MY JOB is to provide for the needs of my wife and children. To do that, I need to derive an income from a job or a family business or a family farm that provides for our material and financial needs and allows us to live honorably. I will leave the task of defining "living honorably" to folks far more qualified than I am, and instead talk about what I know a little something about: family businesses and family farms.

I am 61 years old and have been working in family businesses and also on family farms since I was nine. At one time or another I have owned a construction company, a real estate company, a restaurant, a nightclub, a band, a small manufacturing company, a small distribution business, and a convenience store. I've just about always owned my own business and worked for myself. Since 1982, my business has been *selling* businesses, or "business brokerage." Over that time, I've sold or managed the sale of small businesses in almost every kind of industry, including retail, service, manufacturing, distribution, restaurants, lounges, coin laundries, liquor stores, convenience stores, and franchises of all sorts, all of which were family businesses.

When I started as a business broker 22 years ago, most folks had never heard of it, myself included. One of my hopes in writing this book is that it will help you understand the real value of small business to you, and to all of us, because America is moving back to small business in a huge way. History tends to repeat itself, and more and more folks are returning to self-employment to earn a living. My life mirrors that.

I grew up in a small town in lower South Carolina, called Allendale, about 90 miles west of Charleston. In the 1950s, everyone in town either owned a small family business, a family farm, or worked for someone who did. There were no "big businesses" in Allendale, and there still aren't. My father and all the folks I knew provided for their families by owning and operating their own businesses or farms. Although I didn't realize it at the time, that lifestyle was a great education and training ground for one of the most exciting and necessary businesses in America today—business brokerage.

Basically, you can work for someone else or you can work for yourself; one way or another you have to make a living. My suggestion is that it is best, although not always easiest, to work for yourself, and that means owning your own business (or farm).

The Family Farm

Actually, when you think about it, a family business of any kind is akin to a family farm. I say this because, essentially, their function is the same. That function is to provide for the needs of the owner's family materially and financially. In the world of work, you can work for yourself or you can work for someone else; the needed result is the same, you *must* have an income. You must have an income so you can pay the house payment, car payment, electric and telephone bills; so you can feed, clothe, and educate your children. I've noticed that children all want to eat at least three times a day, every day, and girls always need new clothes.

Like the family farm, in a family business you have to decide what to plant, and you have to prepare to plant, plant at the right time, nurture, fertilize, and maintain the crop. You have to keep the weeds and pests at bay, pray for proper weather, then harvest and go to market at the right time, and hope that the market wants or needs and will pay for your crop. Not to mention the struggles to make more income than it cost you to produce the crop.

Also, without openly wishing locusts, droughts, floods, or other adversity on your fellow farmers, you can only hope that your market is not ruined by overproduction of your product, service, or crop. As we all know, competition is healthy only so long as you can stay ahead of it!

In a family business, you not only have to provide a product or service that the marketplace wants or needs and will pay for, but also manage your business so it produces more than it costs to operate. And again, you have to watch for the competition. Hopefully, the business provides for you and your family's material and financial needs—and a good name by virtue of a "farm" managed in a way that contributes positively to the community.

Success Stories

As I have had the opportunity to help my partners grow our business—Sunbelt Business Brokers Network, Inc.—into the largest business brokerage franchise in the world, I've had the chance to travel across America many times by plane, train,

bus, and automobile. Since I do the entire initial broker training for Sunbelt, every week since we started franchising in
1993, I've traveled to a major city in the United States to con-
duct broker training. I go either to Atlanta; Orlando; New
Orleans; Washington, D.C.; New York; Chicago; Minneapolis; Dallas; Houston; Denver; Phoenix; Los Angeles; San Francisco; Portland; or Seattle.

During these journeys, I have had "windshield time" and
"airport time" to put together ideas about the world of business, and I've gained a healthy respect for my fellow "Road
Warriors" whose jobs require a lot of travel.

As a "Roads Scholar," I've learned about businesses and
people in the various cities, had the chance to study the history of many big businesses that started as small businesses,
and also the chance to hear stories about their founders. I've
been to Corbin, Kentucky, where Colonel Harland Sanders
started Kentucky Fried Chicken; to the original Wendy's in
Columbus, Ohio, started by Dave Thomas; to the home of
George Eastman of Eastman Kodak in Rochester, New York;
to Moline, Illinois, the home of John Deere; and out to a small
town in northwest Arkansas called Bentonville, to the original Walton's 5&10, the home of Wal-Mart, now the largest
retailer in the world.

Bentonville is about 15 miles from Lowell, Arkansas,
home of J.B. Hunt Trucking, the country's largest trucking
company, and 20 miles from Springdale, Arkansas, the home
of Tyson Foods, the world's largest chicken company.

I have also been to Atlanta, the "capital of the South,"
where Ted Turner came up with some wild and crazy ideas
about a 24-hour news service on cable television, later to
become CNN, and also bought a mediocre baseball team, the
Atlanta Braves, with the equally crazy notion of making them

"America's Team." And what about his nutty scheme to buy all of those old films at MGM: who was ever going to watch classic movies? Next he'll probably try to get folks to eat buffalo.

The point I'm trying to make is that almost all big businesses started off as a small business, and somehow hit the market right. Many of them began in small towns and cities across the United States. I find the stories—of both the businesses and their owners—fascinating; they are an integral part of the American business history, the essence of what I call "America's Real and Amazing Economic Engine."

Let's explore some of the changes, small and large, that have occurred in the world of business and the world of work and see how they have influenced us, and might well affect our future.

What the Future May Bring

In writing a book or giving a speech, I use what I learned at my Dale Carnegie course in 1970: it is best to write or talk about what you know. Also, the speech or book should be interesting, informative, entertaining, and brief. In fact, what I know about the world of work comes from the observations and experiences that I've had. In sharing these observations, I hope that you may find them to be interesting, informative, entertaining, and brief and of some help as we look at the world of business and work in America during the twentieth century and as we prepare for how we'll provide for our families in the twenty-first century. We'll explore some of the changes, small and large, that have occurred and how those changes have affected and continue to affect us all.

There are millions of what I call "American Business Heroes," by which I mean small business owners, who provide for themselves and their families and provide jobs for millions more. In fact, in the last decade, substantially all of the new job growth has been in small business, while big business continues laying folks off by the tens of thousands.

In 1999 a new program appeared on TV called *Who Wants to Be a Millionaire?* Well, apparently, and not unexpectedly, just about everyone does. There are a lot of books out about how to become a millionaire, most of them concerning investment advice: to entice regular folks to invest in the stock market, real estate, or precious metals. I have always found it interesting that all of those books have one phrase in common: "The best way to become a millionaire, *except by owning your own business, is* . . ." The exception is stated somewhere in the beginning of the text.

This is kind of like saying, "Except for Michael Jordan, who is the best basketball player in history?" If you don't exclude him, Michael Jordan would be everyone's answer. The same is true of the best way to become a millionaire. Own your own business and be in business for yourself; no other method comes close.

Now, most of us will not get to be millionaires; however, we do all have that chance. You will not get to be a millionaire by working for someone else, unless, of course, you have saved $50 to $100 per month religiously since you were 20 years old and invested it at 7 percent interest, compounded, and never touched it until you were 65. Sorry I missed out on that opportunity! I'm already 61, so that course of action is too late for me. And over the last few years we all relearned that investments in the stock market can go down just as they can go up.

Consequently, I believe that you are better off going into business for yourself and working as hard and as smart as you can, using your own learned and God-given talents and abilities to develop a business that provides a service and/or product to which the market responds. You will also provide for your own job security, something that has "gone with the wind" in American big business. You may end up with a business of considerable value to sell when you finally retire—and who knows, you might get to be a millionaire.

In America, we have educated five generations about how to get a job and develop a job skill or management skill to become more marketable. Not surprisingly, after a layoff by a major corporation or the government, you might find special job training or retraining to help you get another job—a job, by the way, that you could be laid off from again a few years down the road. Maybe just trading one job for another is not the best answer.

I believe you are better off working for yourself, and if you are going into business for yourself, I believe with all my heart that you are better off buying an existing business or a franchise with a proven track record of success than starting your own business from scratch.

U.S. Department of Commerce statistics show that 65 to 90 percent of start-up businesses are not in business after five years. On the other hand, 90 to 95 percent of existing businesses that have been in business three years or longer with a successful track record, or a franchise with a successful track record, are still in business after five years. That is a significant lowering of risk of investment and increases chances of continual business success.

In chapters to come, I will explain why those statistics are true, and how to find the right business for you, as well as how to buy it. Also, even with the tremendous changes in the world of work and technology in the last few years, I'll show you how the more things change, the more they stay the same.

Just as I treat "farm" and "business" interchangeably, I also write about my personal life and my business life as one and the same. Every decision I make affects the people closest to me—my family—and no reflection upon my business experience would be complete without including them. My family, immediate and extended, is an integral and wonderful part of my story, as they will be with your story. Realizing that, let's look at the world of work in the early twentieth century.

3

The World of Work Since 1900

Big Business versus Small Business

T HE UNITED STATES is a big country, blessed with natural resources and a diverse and varied population made up of all nationalities, races, creeds, religions, and skills. In the early twentieth century, most folks lived and worked in small towns, on small farms, and in small businesses owned and run by citizens of that town. The entrepreneurial spirit was strong in America.

The usual family unit had a father who worked for himself or for someone else to provide an income for the family, and a mother who worked inside the home, providing for the needs of her husband and children. One-income families were the norm.

The Industrial Revolution and World War I

The beginning of the Industrial Revolution in the late 1800s and the advent of America's involvement in World War I heralded a major transformation in the world of work. The development of giant factories that produced steel, railroads and automobiles, fuel, steamships, telephones, and electricity brought a "sea change" in the way people provided for their family incomes. A man could make more by working for someone else, particularly a big company, than he could by working for himself. The "big company," or the Industrial Age, had begun.

At the turn of the century we were a nation of small farms and shopkeepers; however, the world of work was about to change forever. Men started leaving the farms and small towns to work for big companies which offered wages that far exceeded what they could make in a small business or farm. These cities and factories grew up around transportation hubs of rivers, seaports, or railheads, and folks migrated to them and the jobs that were clustered there. The "work" mission remained the same, however: to provide for the needs of the family.

The explosive growth of big companies created new relationships between the company (employer) and the workers (employees). Organizational structures had to be redefined as levels of management were added to the "organizational chart." People were hired for specific jobs, and the "corporate ladder" was built. John D. Rockefeller's Standard Oil Company led the way to the horizontal and vertical growth that defined big companies. The economies of scale proved beneficial to the company but had many unsuspected side effects for the worker and competitors. There is usually some good and some bad in everything.

The Postwar Economy

After World War I, the banking industry and the new stock market—or equities market—was straining to keep up with the explosive growth of manufacturers, retailers, transportation, fuel, communications, and utilities, and to address the markets created by the demands of such a robust economy. Many became investors and began dreaming of getting rich in the stock market. Continuous investments by an excess of buyers drove the stock prices up, where before the market price was based on the actual value of companies.

Sure enough, the bubble burst. The stock market crashed in 1929, and the Great Depression that ensued permeated throughout the entire nation, impacting virtually every American family and citizen in some way. Unemployment, for the first time, became a major disaster to the family when those thousands of men who wanted and needed to work couldn't find gainful employment. Almost one-third of the employable population couldn't find a job. Many lined up in soup kitchens, and others (hobos, we called them) went from town to town searching for work.

Folks who worked for themselves in small businesses and on small farms were still employed, and so they fared better. They still had their jobs, since they worked for themselves.

For the first time, the federal government became directly involved in the economy and in the providing of jobs; the Roosevelt administration's Works Progress Administration, for example. Congress passed laws that provided for Social Security and unemployment insurance and certain areas of welfare. These programs provided a partial security net to help provide for families and individuals in need, which means all of us at some point or another in our lifetimes.

These measures and the onset of World War II brought America out of the Depression and put nearly everyone back to work in factories, transportation, the military, retailing, distribution, fuel, communications, and utilities. For the first time, women in large numbers went to work outside the home to help meet the needs of a country at war, as well as the needs of their families. America, the American family, and the world of work were again changed forever.

The Economy After World War II

The postwar economy grew even stronger, and with the G.I. Bill, thousands of veterans went back to school and to college to further their educations and make themselves more valuable in the job market. Families were buying their own homes with government loans from the Federal Housing Administration (FHA) or the Veterans Administration (VA), and the American suburbs began to be developed. Everyone wanted a home with a yard, which seemed the best of all worlds: a family farm—or yard—with a job and income instead of crops.

The quality of life was significantly improved for millions of Americans. The hours of the typical job—8 hours a day, 40 hours a week—were better than working for yourself, and the job produced a good, livable wage without having to worry about managing the company and the other workers. The establishment of a floor, or "minimum," wage, often allowed for a higher standard of living than could be obtained by working for oneself or farming, and the "Great American Middle Class" was born.

Soon enough, consumerism was *in*! We all wanted a house, one or two cars, a dishwasher, washing machine and dryer, college education for our children, two-week vacations—and television.

Much to the nation's delight, television brought entertainment and news to America, and as it became available to a mass market, our world became much smaller with that wonderful talking picture box right in our own homes. Television changed our world, and as with most aspects of life, there was some good and some bad in those changes. Basically, America in the 1950s was as it was depicted on TV. Father had a job with a livable wage; Mother ran the house and children. The children were getting an education and eating three times a day. And the three major television networks—ABC, NBC, and CBS—signed off the air with the National Anthem at 11 p.m., sending Americans to sleep. How things change!

The 1960s arrived quietly enough. Most Americans had a good job or worked for themselves, and life seemed to be going pretty well. Big companies were getting even bigger and providing more and more jobs. A young person's goal was to get a good education and get a good job with a big name company. If he or she performed the job well, that was his "job security," and he would stay with the company, possibly in the same position, through retirement. If he was good, he might even move up the corporate ladder of success and at some point retire as an executive, or at least retire as a former employee with some stream of retirement income.

Like a lot of things that seem too good to last, that image of America was about to unravel. Women, African Americans, and other minorities were not sharing in the American Dream. The civil rights movement of the 1960s awoke the nation, and as a result, many (though certainly not all) wrongs slowly began to be righted. Regarding race issues, the grossly false "separate but equal" programs were exposed for being anything but equal, and eventually, opportunities for education, jobs, housing, and advancement were made available to all Americans.

In the 1960s the country was also rocked by the assassination of President John F. Kennedy, followed by the assassination of Dr. Martin Luther King Jr., the civil rights leader, and

Senator Robert Kennedy, a candidate for president. No one who lived through that time remained untouched by those events. Many can remember where they were and what they were doing when the tragedies occurred.

America's military involvement in Vietnam, a little known country in Southeast Asia, escalated from an advisory role to a full-scale but undeclared war involving over 1 million of our finest young people as we tried to prevent a supposed "domino effect"—the spread of communism throughout the Asian world. After 14 years of indecisiveness and the tragic loss of millions of lives, including more than 58,000 Americans, we finally pulled out of South Vietnam, vowing never again to send our young heroes back to war without knowing why we were there.

The 1970s saw a president, Richard Nixon, resign to avoid impeachment in what was dubbed the Watergate affair. We struggled to regain our footings in what had been the American way, and failing that, to just get back to a normal life in a stable and peaceful world. Our absolute trust in government, however, was damaged forever.

We continued to move to the cities as small farms were lost to development and were unable to compete with large "corporate farms" run by management teams with lots of capital. Small businesses also had a difficult time competing with big corporate businesses, which were encroaching on their territory and increasingly competing for the same customers. The world of work and small business was changing yet again.

The Rise of Big Business

Until now most big businesses were in manufacturing, retailing, distribution, transportation, government contracting, oil, utilities, communications, and—in cities—television. Small towns and suburbs were safe havens for small business retailers and service providers who owned and operated their own businesses. Gas station owner/operators represented big companies on-site, and financing was done by local banks (banks were not allowed to cross state lines). Automobile companies like General Motors, Ford, and Chrysler had "local" dealers who were small business people. Consequently, in many ways, big business and small business had somewhat of a partnership, and each had its own defined role and location in the marketplace.

Giant retailers began to creep into the suburbs of large cities with the development of shopping centers and shopping malls that followed the market of customers as they migrated from urban areas to suburbia. Sears, Montgomery Ward, J.C. Penney, and a discount retailer named Kmart began aggressively moving into the suburbs, creating shopping districts and providing opportunities for small support businesses such as card shops, gift shops, restaurants, hair salons, and dry cleaners.

In order to "keep up with the Joneses'" standard of living, in more and more families the wife sought employment outside of the home, and two family incomes became the norm, rather than the exception. In addition to "traditional" women's jobs such as teaching, health care, and secretarial support, women were becoming business executives, doctors, lawyers, and business owners.

Once women got a taste of their own income and independence, there was no turning back. Today, women are involved successfully and positively in all aspects of business and other professions, including the military. They are doing an outstanding job, even at such male bastions as The Citadel, the military college of South Carolina. Contrary to popular belief in Charleston at the time, the walls did not fall down when women were admitted. (Since I am a 1965 graduate of The Citadel, I feel I can comment on the subject with some authority!)

Two more major changes were developing in America that would have a revolutionary impact on the world of business and work. A milk-shake appliance salesman named Ray Kroc and a nice retired motel owner and restaurateur from Corbin, Kentucky, who had a chicken recipe that everyone loved, started a fast-food phenomenon that led to a business revolution called *franchising*. This phenomenon is still having a major impact on the world of work, and allowing a lot of folks to go back into business "for themselves but not by themselves."

The second major change started in a small town in Arkansas northwest of the Ozark Mountains with a store named Walton's 5&10. Although the population of the town of Bentonville is still only about 10,000, the company, Wal-Mart, is the largest retailer in the world, with over $220 billion in annual sales. It has over 4,380 stores, employs over 1.28 million people, and has had a major impact on work and small business in virtually every city and town in America. Recently, Wal-Mart surpassed General Motors as the company with the highest gross sales in the world. Only Exxon-Mobil had higher gross sales, and in 2001, Wal-Mart overtook them as well.

Add a few of the other major, aggressive retailers like Home Depot, Lowe's, Staples, Office Depot, The Limited, Gap, and franchises or multiple outlet stores like McDonald's, Burger King, Subway, Taco Bell, Applebee's, Chili's, Olive Garden, Ruby Tuesdays, TGI Fridays, Ace Hardware, Pep Boys, Precision Tune, Ammco Transmission, One Hour Martinizing, Fast Signs, Deck the Walls, etc., and you will see how big business and franchising have permeated every aspect of business, large and small, in towns of all sizes across America.

Another quantum leap that has greatly impacted our world is the advancement of technology. It is now possible to watch television 24 hours a day, choosing from a menu of hundreds of channels. Further, and perhaps the biggest of all modern developments, are personal computers, the Internet, and the World Wide Web. Wow!!! We've just begun to see the changes that technology will produce and/or demand. Every business around the globe is affected by this technology; indeed, the richest folks in America today can thank these changes in technology, and the response of the marketplace to them, for their good fortune.

Downsizing

With the 1980s came a robust economy, and as big business sought ways to compete and succeed in a fast-changing world, a new management phenomenon, called "reengineering," "downsizing," or "rightsizing," was born—terms that have become code words for firing people. If you're one of the tens of thousands who have been "downsized," the literal translation is: "You ain't got a job anymore."

It's a little more complicated than that, of course, but the net results are the same: for the first time in some people's adult lives, they don't have a job. The old idea of getting a good job with a big company, doing well, having job security, and working with that company until retirement is a concept that is gone forever. When was the last time you heard the phrase, "Move up the corporate ladder"?

One thing that makes this change so personal and disconcerting is that it doesn't matter how good a job you've done, when the company merges, reengineers, offshores jobs, or is acquired by another company, you might expect to hear what Ted Turner told his son, who was working for CNN at the time it was acquired by Time Warner and was hoping to stay on after the merger: "Son, you're toast."

The world of work has been turned upside down in America—job security is gone and is not coming back. This is another huge change in the world of work, just as big as the Industrial Revolution's impact on the nineteenth and twentieth centuries, only in reverse. A good lesson for dealing with some of these changes can be found in Dr. Spencer Johnson's excellent book, *Who Moved My Cheese?*

Across America the workplace has eliminated hundreds of thousands of jobs—over 1.8 million in 2001 alone. Educated, experienced people who want and need to work are unemployed for the first time. Their "American Dream Job" is gone, and it will remain gone. Now that the income from the job has stopped, guess what has not stopped? The house payment, car payments, the children's education bills . . . And everyone still wants to eat three times a day.

Think back with me a few years. If you find a dictionary over 11 years old, the words *reengineering, downsizing, rightsizing,* and *offshoring* are not included. Back then, if a major company had announced that they were laying off 10,000 of their key people, what would have happened to their stock? It would have *dropped like a rock*, devastating the company and the community, as well as the 10,000 people who were laid off. Since reengineering, the stock market reaction to a layoff of several thousand is *positive* and the stock *goes up*! What's wrong with this picture?

To show an example of this phenomenon, I'll share with you a 1994 *Wall Street Journal* article on the Xerox Corporation I cut out and saved. Now, this is not a criticism of Xerox, which incidentally I consider to be a wonderful company that may or may not survive, but it illustrates my point. The headline announces: "Xerox to cut 10,000 jobs, shut facilities, changes of $854 million are planned; net loss is likely for the full year." Approximately four paragraphs into the story it reads: "The magnitude of the new reductions caught some analysts by surprise; Xerox shares surged $5.625, or 7 percent, to close at $86.375 in composite trading on the New York Stock Exchange."

Do you know that Xerox shares have never jumped 7 percent in one day with the announcement of any new equipment, technical advancement, managerial change, or profit statement? But here they announce the firing of 10,000 people and the stock jumps 7 percent—great for the shareholders, but not necessarily for the 10,000 ex-employees.

Realizing that one of management's main jobs is to enhance shareholder value, then, from the management and shareholder perspective, if it gets the stock up, it's good business to fire a few thousand people. If you can lay off 10,000 people and get the stock market to react with an upward spike, you might ask: Why doesn't every big company lay off 10,000 people? Well, they have, and they will again as long as the stock market's reaction is positive.

Another little known but important aspect of reengineering is hidden in the glamour of the bull market that generally spanned the 1985–1999 time period. The reengineering ploy resulted in tax consequences for employee layoffs, and the numbers are staggering. Here's how it works: In order to manage the layoffs to prevent a "riot in the street" in the community—as well as all the unpleasant publicity that might follow—corporations give bonuses to the "voluntary" downsized, kind of like throwing a dog a bone to keep it from barking. Now, when you lay off 10,000 people and give them $40,000 retirement bonuses, where do you think the $400 million comes from? You guessed it, the U.S. taxpayer. Through what is called NOL—net operating loss—a loss can carry back for three years or carry forward for up to 15 years.

In other words, the company strategy was to create a loss of $400 million through the layoff and then refile the tax returns for the past three years and "get back" any taxes paid over the last three years and/or shelter profits forward. They sometimes made more money creating that loss than they did making and selling their products. Remember when the headlines read, "Changes of $854 million are planned, net losses likely for a full year"? *Likely*, my a_ _ (three letter word for derriere)!

There was a three-year period, in fact, when you couldn't pick up a business periodical that did not have a major article about reengineering, downsizing, or rightsizing. It took me a while to put the puzzle pieces together. The U.S. deficit in 1983, for the first time in America's history, was $1 trillion; by 1986 it was $2 trillion; in 1989, $3 trillion; in 1992, $4 trillion; and now it is a staggering $7 trillion. One of the largest contributors to that amount has been the reengineering of corporate tax returns, coupled with the reduced withholding from employees.

Our political debates are all about taxing and spending. The Democrats blame the deficit on the Republicans, and the Republicans blame the Democrats, and the Congress blames the president, and the president blames Congress. Actually, we are ALL somewhat guilty: we want them to balance the budget but not cut our favorite programs. And the ever-increasing interest cost of the deficit only adds to the problems.

The main causes and effects of big business's financials are rarely discussed because they are too complicated for a 30-second sound bite, and we live in a 30-second-sound-bite world. If you ask someone, "Don't you think G.E. should pay its fair share of taxes?" the 30-second answer is, "Well, if they had to pay more taxes, they'd just pass that on to us in higher costs for services. So we'd end up paying it one way or another." End of 30-second answer—when actually it is much more complicated than that.

The huge deficits came not from the political debate about changes in taxing and spending, but from big companies getting back all the taxes that they had paid through planned, management-created tax losses, and we were trying to fill up a bucket with no bottom. Every big company that had a major layoff got back millions of dollars in taxes that they had paid or sheltered future profits. Maybe someone ought to put a plug in the bucket so there is no tax advantage to laying off 10,000 people.

Since 1985 hundreds of thousands of employees have been downsized, and their jobs are not coming back. In the '50s, '60s, and '70s, when a big company laid off workers, especially key people, they couldn't wait to hire them back. Today they not only won't hire them back, they can't wait to fire more if the stock results are positive. Now, layoffs are so commonplace that they no longer have to give "golden parachute" bonuses to soften the blow or throw the doggie a bone to keep a worker quiet. They just lay him off.

The public corporate management mentality has changed. Where once the employees and customers were the most important asset of the business, now the stock value is the most important thing, which drives a lot of management's decisions. I think it is a shortsighted and a wrong-sided approach that will backfire—as "Chainsaw Al" Dunlap found out. Add to that the major shifts in jobs and layoffs due to "robotics" and better computer technology in general, and thousands of additional jobs are eliminated. Machines do not require sick leave, health insurance, or retirement programs. It used to be that whenever a company opened a $300 million plant, 3,000 to 4,000 people were hired to run it. Nowadays, they have 60 to 100 people employed in the whole plant. They call it better productivity, which might sound good but translates into fewer jobs.

Offshoring

Another major business trend that we see affecting the world of work in America is globalization and the offshoring of jobs to other countries with lower cost employees. You cannot stop a market-driven trend or the laws of economics; however, you must identify such factors and realize how they are influencing your environment.

A little over two years ago I was doing a two-day broker training program in the Sunbelt office in Rochester, New York. We were also doing a seminar on the advantages of buying an existing business or franchise at the Chamber of Commerce building because Xerox had recently announced a layoff of 6,500 employees. Rochester is the "imaging capital of the world," being the headquarters of Eastman Kodak, Xerox, and the now bankrupt company formerly known as Polaroid. On the credenza in the Rochester Sunbelt office was a recent copy of the *Rochester Business Journal*. I picked it up and took a look at an article that shocked me. It told the story of the cost of producing a sophisticated imaging system at Eastman Kodak called "The Professional."

Now, I have no idea what The Professional system is—perhaps a medical application or something—but here were the numbers: To produce The Professional in Rochester cost $55,300. Do you know how much it cost to produce it in mainland China? A minor $1,400. Wow. Some difference!

Where do think that they are going to produce The Professional? You guessed it. The laws of economics are brutal. In the real world, Eastman Kodak cannot say, "By George, we are a great company and Rochester is a great company town, so we are going to keep jobs for our loyal employees here in Rochester and we will always produce The Professional here in the good ol' U.S.A." No matter how much they would like to be able to promise that, they can't, or the company could go broke. Kodak is forced to produce at the lowest price or someone else will. Also, with the technology change to digital imaging, Kodak does not need as many employees to process film. Thousands and thousands of jobs have been lost in the United States due to changes in the global market and technology, and this was happening long before NAFTA.

Well, I am from South Carolina, so I cannot say this out loud; however, we are bemoaning the loss of thousands of textile jobs to Mexico and China. Guess what? We "stole" that entire industry from "up North" 100 years ago because of our low-cost labor compared to labor union wages—now it is happening to us and we are not happy about it.

Consider Japan, for another example of the amazing shift in the world of economics and employment. When we were growing up and the world seemed simpler, products produced in Japan cost about half of "American made" products, and products from Taiwan or Korea cost even less. How things change.

Japan is now a net importing country. Just a few short years ago one of America's largest economic problems was its trade imbalance with Japan—the Japanese economy was so strong that it appeared they were buying up America. Now look what's happened to Japan's economy. Things have reversed. Where does Japan manufacture its automobiles? In the United States or in mainland China, where the labor costs are one-tenth what they are in Japan. Japan's economy is in serious jeopardy. They are financing some houses for 105 years to make the numbers work. The world of work and the world's model of job security has turned on its head.

Now our trade imbalance is with China. Their huge population and low wage scale has resulted in a flood of products to the United States, and they are ending up with tons of U.S. dollars that they are using to buy our debt. Yes, China is financing our deficit. So obviously, Nixon was not the "only guy" who could go to China—no wonder George Bush Sr. threw up: he must have seen this coming.

What History Says to Us Now

So, all in all, I believe that you are better off creating your own job security by going into business for yourself and running your business successfully. The family business has become the family farm, just as the family farm has become the family business: it has to be done here, where you live. The jobs that are offered by a faceless company are somewhat less attractive. America has truly been blessed—we're big, we're strong, we're free, and we're educated. We are the world's largest producer of goods and services, and also the world's largest market for goods and services. I absolutely believe the old adage that as long as "America is good, America will be great."

Following the unprovoked, senseless, and cowardly act against the United States by terrorists in New York City, Pennsylvania, and Washington, D.C., on September 11, 2001, we have strengthened our security and provoked a national unity not seen since World War II. We are a strong nation under God, and we will continue to get stronger.

Just how this "war on terrorism" will unfold is uncertain, except as to its eventual outcome. We will prevail. Just how these events will affect the world of small business and the world of work is not clear except that in the short term it has exacerbated the job loss of big companies as they adjust to new market conditions, real and perceived. I believe that many of these laid-off employees would be far better off going into business for themselves, rather than just seeking another job.

As the world changes, excluding the terrible tragedies of 9/11 and the wars in Afghanistan and Iraq, I believe some of the changes are good for America's people. We're heading back to being a nation of shopkeepers and farmers, or in today's terms, small businessmen and businesswomen who are fiercely independent, who provide for their own job security and for their families by owning and managing their own businesses. They are building their financial portfolios by investing in themselves.

We are in the business of retail, service, manufacturing, distribution, restaurants, lounges, coin laundries, dry cleaners, liquor stores, auto repair, multilevel marketing, franchise companies, professional consultancies—and independent businesses of all types. The structure of the business may be a sole proprietorship, a partnership, or a corporation of some definition—such as a C or an S corporation, or a hybrid like an LLC, which combines some of the characteristics of the

C and the S. But in essence it's the small privately owned business—or mom-and-pop business, as it is sometimes referred to—that provides the same necessities as a job does for you and your family. These businesses provide an income for the owner, and they allow them to provide for their needs and the needs of their families.

4

My Life in Business

WHEN I WAS GROWING UP in Allendale, my dad was a small businessman in the community. He was a good, honest, hardworking, decent, smart, and reasonably successful small-town businessman. Everyone in Allendale respected my father, many sought his advice, particularly in business matters, and there was never any question that Mr. Ben's word was his bond. He provided for my charming and sweet mother, my older brother Ben, my younger sister Lois, and myself, and he gave us a good name. He was my hero.

Whether he was a farmer, banker, produce broker, inventor, tractor company dealer, motel owner, or restaurant owner—all of which he was at some stage of his adult life—he managed the business successfully. He never was a millionaire, but he was always successful. He was a wonderful father, and quite frankly, all I ever wanted was to be like him. Going through some of Dad's effects after he passed away in 1989, I found a note that he had kept since I was in the seventh grade. My teacher, Mrs. Margaret Boylston, asked us one day to write a short paragraph in class about "our ambition." This is what I wrote:

My ambition is this . . .

I want to try for all I am worth to be as good a
man as my father is. I want to try to live up to the good
name he has made for his family and himself. I want to
make something out of life as he does and is still doing.
I want to help him in his business. This will be a very
hard task, but if I work hard enough, maybe someday
my dream and my "ambition" will come true.

—Ed Pendarvis, 1956

Unbeknownst to me, the teacher had sent this note to my
father and he kept it for the rest of his life. I haven't seemed
to change much in the fifty years since then. I am still trying
to live up to my dad and fulfill "My Ambition."

In Allendale, like other small towns, everyone either
owned a small farm or small business or worked for someone
who did. It was a great place to grow up. Business never
strayed far from its traditional path, and even the elected offi-
cials discouraged any big business or plants from relocating
to Allendale because it might take workers away from the
small businesses and farms. Folks pretty much liked things
the way they were.

Because U.S. Highway 301 went through Allendale, and
at that time was the major north-south route from Maine to
Florida, we had 13 motels in our little town. With a population of only 3,500, we had a Holiday Inn, Howard Johnson,
and Quality Courts (which Dad owned), and many indepen-
dents. Big farmers and motel/restaurant owners and bankers
were the wealthiest folks in town.

In the late 1950s the federal government built the Savannah River Project, or the "bomb plant," as we in the coun-
ties of Allendale, Barnwell, and Aiken called it. It was the first

"big company" to come to our area. The plant began hiring thousands of folks for higher wages than could be made at a small business or farm, and everyone wanted one of those government jobs. Things were beginning to change.

My first job, at age nine, was counting watermelons for Dad in the summer when the farmhands would load tractor-trailer trucks or railroad cars full of watermelons to ship north to the market, where the "Yankees" paid a lot for fresh fruit. The third season, however, I was walking down to the produce shed one morning when Tom Keller, a prominent motel owner, asked me if I would like to be a bellhop at his motel every afternoon after school. He said he would pay me a dollar per day, plus tips.

At the age of 11, I resigned from farm work and headed for the bright lights, and better hours and cash, of the Allendale Motel. I've never looked back. In four years, I never missed a day of work except for the four days I was sick. Every afternoon from 3 to 8 p.m., seven days a week, I was there and made pretty good money for a kid my age, and I had no overhead. I was supposed to share a rotation of customers with the owner's son, Tommy, as they arrived at the motel. Tommy was older, had his own car and a girlfriend. She'd come over every afternoon and they'd sit out in the car and listen to the radio and talk. Consequently, I got to take almost *all* the guests of the motel to their rooms. I learned two things that were pretty important: (1) be nice, polite, and helpful to people and you'll get good tips; and (2) don't let girlfriends get in the way of making money.

When I was 15, Dad bought the Quality Courts Motel, and I went to work for him. I worked there through high school as a bellhop and later ran the office. I learned two things from that job: (1) you actually make more money as a bellhop than you do running the desk; and (2) you sometimes don't make as much money working for your family as you do working for someone else.

In 1961, after graduating from Allendale-Fairfax High School with a slightly better grade in football than in academics, I enrolled in The Citadel, the Military College of South Carolina. The first four years there were the most unpleasant; after that (since it was only a four-year school!), it wasn't so bad.

I went out for football my freshman year, but soon learned that although I had been a fairly good player in high school, I was too slow and too small to play college football. I'm not the brightest bear in the woods, but I do know that the avoidance of pain is normally the better track, and I quickly realized that professional football was not in my career plans. I made a decision to quit the team and try to find another path to enrich my life at The Citadel. Looking for any activity that would get me out of Friday afternoon parades and help me find an individual niche in a world where everyone wore the same uniform, ate the same food, and shared the same schedule, I signed up to sell advertising for *The Sphinx*, The Citadel yearbook.

I liked selling ads. It was a lot less painful than football, and I believed in the value of folks supporting The Citadel. By my junior year I had sold more ads than anyone ever had, so they made me advertising editor. I asked Colonel McAllister, the administrative dean, who was one of the finest gentlemen I have ever met, to help me get permission from The Citadel to put together a staff of ad salesmen. As motivation for my sales team, I convinced Colonel McAllister to authorize a short weekend leave (release) away from The

Citadel each time a salesman sold at least $250 worth of advertising.

I learned two things: (1) if you get the right program going and the support of your superiors, you can accomplish a great deal; and (2) if you offer a Citadel cadet a weekend leave for $250 worth of advertising, you can sell $10,000 of advertising space in three months.

My academic record at college was, again, not outstanding; however, by the grace of God, I finally graduated with a gentleman's C and some of the most beautiful Ds in physics and chemistry that you have ever seen.

I had some wonderful classmates in the class of 1965. We formed an effective underground organization affectionately called "Fun, Inc." Every member of our class chipped in a few bucks and we rented a beach house at Folly Beach—something that was absolutely against The Citadel's policy. Our organization had a board of directors made up of one officer and one senior private from each of the 17 companies at The Citadel. We even made the man who lived across the street from the beach house and the police chief of Folly Beach honorary members of our class. The reason, of course, was to keep them from calling Gen. Mark Clark, the president of The Citadel, or Col. Courvousie, "The Boo," to tell them about our escapade. As a final nod to the law, we hired off-duty policemen to help direct traffic whenever we had a party. This organizational structure of one officer and one senior private later became the official structure of the senior class board of directors, which still functions well at The Citadel.

With good friends supporting me, I was honored by being elected the class president, and even though I seemed to be playing catch-up in my grades (I didn't graduate until August because of an unnamed physics professor), I was, for some mysterious reason, voted "Most Likely to Succeed" by my classmates. Go figure!

During our thirtieth reunion in 1995, the school was having the battle of its life. It seems that over $10 million was spent in legal fees trying to prevent women from entering The Citadel. Quite frankly, on that issue I probably differed from some of my Citadel buddies in that I had spent four years trying to get a woman *into* the barracks. Everyone was now nervously saying, "The women are coming, the women are coming." Now, what's wrong with this picture?

Incidentally, a wonderful and successful author and storyteller, Pat Conroy, has written several books about life at The Citadel and growing up in the South Carolina low country. He was two years behind me at school, graduating in the class of 1967. Pat has a great command of the English language and can paint a magnificent picture with "words that are worth a thousand pictures." Many of his books have been made into films. This is a great example of being successful at doing what you like.

After college, I spent two years on active duty in the U.S. Army field artillery. The army sent me to the Republic of Korea, rather than the Republic of Vietnam, for 13 months. It was a great tour of duty, and I learned a lot about the Korean people and their country. Then my duty rotation sent me to Fort Benning, Georgia, where I worked my way into Ranger School, which almost killed me! Great training, but if I ever go back into the mountains of north Georgia, it is going to be as a tourist.

Now it was time to enter the world of work. I had always wanted to go into business with my dad, but it just didn't work out that way. When I got out of the army in 1967, Dad wasn't interested in expanding the motel business, and the Eisenhower Interstate Project was building a highway called Interstate 95, stretching from Maine to Florida. It was rumored that it would take most, if not all, of the traffic off of Highway 301. We didn't believe that it would, but it did.

In Allendale, as in many South Carolina towns, the motel and restaurant business died a quick death after Interstate 95 opened. I learned two things: (1) a major change in a market trend can put you out of business no matter how smart you are or how hard you work; and (2) you cannot stop or change a market trend.

In 1969, after working with Dad about a year, I decided that I had to move to Columbia, South Carolina (the state capital), or Charleston (the capital of charm and grace). I chose Charleston, and I'm glad I did. I called a bright, young, aggressive real estate developer and homebuilder whom I had met in Charleston, Arthur Ravenel Jr., and asked to meet with him about a possible job. Mr. Ravenel was kind enough to give me an interview, and I went there determined to get a job and learn the real estate and construction business from him. I offered to work for nothing for six months if he would teach me the business. Then, at the end of six months, I would stay on with him, or not, depending on what he or I wanted at that time. At the end of six months he was kind enough to offer me a job at $1,000 per month working as the vice president of the company.

I enjoyed working for Mr. Ravenel, later to be Congressman Ravenel and State Senator Ravenel, and one of the most effective public servants I have ever known. One of his favorite sayings, "Nothing beats a failure, like a TRY," is a simple, but brutally accurate statement that has helped me persevere on many occasions when things just didn't seem to be working. However pleasurable working for him was, when I had the opportunity, in 1973, to go into business for myself, I took it and never looked back.

In 1972 four men who were all millionaires (at least on paper), started a 160-unit luxury condominium development at Snee Farm Country Club in Mt. Pleasant, South Carolina, a beautiful suburb of Charleston. They were about 50 percent complete with Phase I of the development of Ventura Villas— the first 32 units, swimming pool, tennis courts, land acquisition, and site work—when the managing partner had a heart attack and died.

Each of the four men and their wives were personally signed on to a $4.5 million construction loan with a REIT (Real Estate Investment Trust) out of Silver Spring, Maryland. The interest rate was prime plus 5 percent, and the monthly payments of interest, at that time, were running over $20,000 per month. These had to be paid or the REIT would not disperse the construction draw to the contractor.

Since the managing partner who died was the only one of the four owners who had been in the construction and real estate business, the remaining owners had both a major management problem and a major cash flow problem. They couldn't, or wouldn't, come up with the interest payments, so the REIT stopped dispersing the construction draws, and the contractor, MB Kahn Construction Company of Columbia, was threatening to shut down the job.

They needed $75,000 immediately to pay the back interest so the REIT loan would be made current. They would then disperse the construction draw, allowing the building to be completed. The owners were desperately trying to sell 25 percent of the project to anyone who had lots of money and real estate and/or development experience. To that end, they showed the project to every rich person in town who would listen to them.

At that time, there were only nine houses in the Snee Farm development (currently, there are around 1,000) and no one in Charleston could even spell "condominium" or figure out exactly what an "air lot" was (including me). However, I was invited to talk to the owners on behalf of my boss, Arthur Ravenel. He had money and didn't want to lose it, and said that he wouldn't touch the project with a 10-foot pole. He felt it had too many "hooks" in it and too many problems.

There were two slight differences between me and everyone else who looked at the project: (1) they had a great deal of money, but didn't want the project; and (2) I wanted the project, but—and it was a big but—I didn't have $75,000. I had about $3,000 in savings; I was a "little short," as we called that condition in Charleston.

I'll never forget that time in my life: I didn't sleep for three days, operating on sheer adrenaline. I kept looking at the project and running my numbers. There wasn't anyone in the world who was going to lend me $4.5 million to build a development, but the loan was already made. I didn't need the entire $4.5 million, I just needed $75,000. So, where could I get $75,000? I went to see Dad.

Now, my dad was a smart businessman, and he was way too smart to lend me $75,000. However, because of my enthusiasm and the location, plus my four years experience in real estate and construction, Dad and a family friend (a big farmer in Allendale, Henry Wingo) agreed to lend me the money. All of a sudden I was a player.

Out of this experience I learned three things: (1) finding someone who wants what you're selling is a lot more important than just dealing with folks who have a lot of money and don't want what you're selling; (2) don't ever try to qualify someone only by how much money they have—if they want something bad enough, they may find the money; and (3) it's probably best not to buy something that's already killed one guy.

Well, we had some times. Mr. Ravenel was right: there were lots and lots of hooks, some with pretty sizable and very mean "barbs." The first three problems that showed up was that the owners hadn't arranged for any permanent financing to "take out" the construction loans, and, as I mentioned earlier, nobody in Charleston in 1973 could spell condominium, much less make a 30-year permanent loan on an air lot.

The second problem we ran into was that we had some cost "overruns" that had to be paid for by the developers outside of the construction loans by the REIT. That bill was already over $110,000 and growing (the other owners had neglected to tell me about that).

The third unpleasantness was that when we four "owners" had to come up with the next month's interest payments of $22,000, the "other" millionaires shared with me the fact that they didn't have any more money. To say that I wasn't having a very good day would be a little short of an understatement, and I was beginning to get a clearer picture as to why the original partner left.

It seemed as though several people were getting upset about not being paid, and I started having dreams about things like tap-dancing in a minefield. Telephone calls were not always happy occasions, and some folks began to think that I might not make it. The one thing that helped was that I kept in touch with everyone and worked as hard as I could to get the project open: if we couldn't get Phase I open and start selling, we would be dead in the water.

We had set up two model homes for exhibits to show prospective buyers finished and furnished units, and my wife Susanne, stepdaughters Stephanie and Elizabeth, and I moved into a third unit that we used as a third model. I spent every waking hour and most of my sleeping hours trying to build, sell, close, finance, or refinance the project.

Sometimes little unexpected things help in a big way. Susanne and I took a "honeymoon" trip to Silver Spring, Maryland, to allow me to meet our REIT lenders for the first time and propose some restructuring of our loan arrangements. There was no way to pay the interest payments monthly and still have funds to get the project open. I desperately needed whatever money I could scrape together to do marketing brochures and get the road paved.

Well, during a somewhat tense part of my opening statement about the state of the project to the president and vice president of the REIT, on the twelfth floor of an office building in Silver Spring, sitting at the largest boardroom table I had ever seen, a receptionist walked into the boardroom with some information the president had asked for. Of course, I stood up (a lady had entered the room!). Everyone else was a little taken aback.

The men and the woman were impressed with my manners, if not my lack of capital, and they agreed to a moratorium on interest payments until some date in the future. They also reluctantly agreed to lend me another $275,000 to start another building to show "movement" of the project. We now had some breathing room and some momentum.

Out of that experience I learned two things: (1) it is important to have good manners; and (2) when you're dealing with a bank, it's far better if they already have millions of dollars invested in a project and you can convince them that you are their best hope of getting it back.

While we had some challenging times (again, a little bit of an understatement), we continued to try to sell condominiums. Two other unexpected circumstances—out of a combination of hard work and pure dumb luck—helped to save us.

With my marriage to Susanne, in addition to a wonderful new family I also got a riding lawn mower, which I used to cut the grass at Ventura Villas. (Did I mention that I was the developer, builder, salesman, maintenance man, yard boy, painter, and security guard?) One Saturday morning as I was cutting the grass, a blue Ford pulled into the condo area. I got off of the lawn mower, got into one of the two used golf carts I had purchased to make us look like a resort, and rode over to pick up the potential buyers. I always showed everyone through the model homes personally.

As was usually the case, I showed this gentleman and his wife the two models and our home, which as I said served as the third model. They were impressed with my family and our "hands on" involvement in the project. When they started to leave, the gentleman asked me if this was a project funded by an REIT out of Silver Spring, and I said, "Yes, sir." Well, it turned out he was Cary Winston, chairman of the board of the REIT in Silver Spring. And it happened that he was then kind enough to speak for me whenever they considered foreclosing on us, saying something like, "We couldn't find anyone else who would work as hard as that fellow and his family at Ventura Villas to make the project successful." They had faith that through our persistence, perseverance, hard work, total commitment, and luck, I would eventually pay them off. We had some trying times, to say the least, but they never foreclosed, and they eventually did get their money back.

The other major problem at the time was that we could not get any local banks or savings and loans to give us any construction loans or 30-year mortgages, since these institutions were convinced we were going to fail. The president, vice president, and chief loan officers of First Federal Savings and Loan, the largest S&L in Charleston, were kind enough to let me make a presentation to them about borrowing some money. The meeting, in which I presented my construction plan and business plan, lasted over an hour and a half. They smiled, listened politely, asked a few questions, and when I was finished, the president, Howard Burkey, gave me a ballpoint pen with the First Federal logo printed on it and a "token" to get out of the parking lot. They still couldn't spell condominium.

Some more encouraging help and hope came from one of the first residents of Ventura Villas—Bill Moore and his wife, Jackie, from Columbia, South Carolina. They had bought one of the villas for cash (he was a big-time investor or something). One day he walked into my construction office and said, "Captain Ed"—he always called me that, for some reason— "how much do you need to build one of these buildings?"

I said, "About $275,000."

He pulled out a cashier's check for $375,000 that he had just received on some deal and said, "Captain Ed, I'll lend you $275,000 for six months at 20 percent interest, discounted, to build a building, but you've got to pay me back promptly in six months or I will own it."

I thought about that for all of about three seconds and then said, "I'll tell you what—you let me put the entire amount in First Federal Savings and Loan in my name for the six months and draw down against it and I'll do it."

It was a deal!

I put $275,000 in First Federal in my name, and all of a sudden the bank thought I was doing great. The old adage that "a bank will gladly lend you money if you don't need it" comes to mind. The bank agreed to make some permanent, 30-year "take-out" loans and agreed to lend me $275,000 to construct another building of eight units. And then we had two new buildings under construction, and Henry Heinsohn at State Savings and Loan agreed to lend me another $275,000 to start a third building.

As we got closer to the six-month deadline, I had four of the eight units under contract of sale, and when the Cooper River Federal Savings and Loan agreed to refinance that building, I paid Bill Moore back within a week of his deadline. We started selling condos, and built and sold the rest of the project somewhat successfully over the next several years. A major factor in my survival during that part of my life was my good friend and attorney, Bill Ackerman. His advice and guidance was invaluable.

When Susanne and I got married, she was a widow, and I got a wonderful new family of her and her two daughters, Stephanie (4 years old) and Elizabeth (2 years old). Then in 1976, the greatest event in my life happened with the birth of our daughter Sara. Now, I had three wonderful daughters, since I adopted Stephanie and Elizabeth. Basically, everything seemed to be going well; however, something called inflation and rising interest rates were about to become major problems for all businesses, and the real estate industry in particular.

It became increasingly difficult to operate the business, since the cost of construction, like the cost of energy and the cost of money, began to break everybody, myself included. From 1980 to 1982, as interest rates hovered around 18.5 to won't do well in something you don't like—it will be tough enough even if you do like it.

During the two years that I worked with my partner, we had some terrific highs and lows. At one point we decided to reopen a restaurant and lounge in Charleston, similar to the one he'd successfully run before, called the Harbor House. "You can never go home again" comes to mind, since the venture was a financial disaster. I ended up having to buy my partner out of the brokerage business for one dollar and take on the assumption of tens of thousands of dollars in losses in both businesses and a severe shortage in our bank accounts. Had my brother Ben and sister Lois not helped me out with loans, I would have never made it. From this I learned two things: (1) when you think you have a problem with a partner, you probably do; and (2) don't ever let someone else run your checkbook. (Underline number 2.)

Also in 1984, I ran for Congress from the First Congressional District of South Carolina as a Democrat in the most Republican election in South Carolina history. I sold my business, NL Business Brokers, to make the race for Congress, and so I could put all my efforts into trying to win. The only buyer that understood business brokerage in Charleston was my only (and larger) competitor in the city, a company called Sunbelt Business Brokers.

Despite my hard-fought campaign, the voters, in their wisdom, decided that I made a better business broker than a congressman, and they voted overwhelmingly for me to return to the field of business brokerage. I received a mandate from the public to stay in business! So I went back to work with Sunbelt Business Brokers as a broker-agent, and over the span of three years I bought out the ownership interest of the other three partners, one by one.

During this time of economic turmoil and overextended civic activity and politics, which commanded all of my time, energy, and money, something got shortchanged in my life: my marriage. Susanne and I divorced, and I found solace and stability by focusing on business. I believe that helping folks sell or buy businesses is what I was sent here to do. I like working with sellers, learning about them and their businesses and what's going on in their lives that makes them interested in selling. I call it their business story.

Most of the time, the reason for selling is human-driven—for instance, the owner may be retiring, in poor health, has died, or is getting a divorce, relocating, wants to do something else, or is just burned out or tired of the business. I like to think of it in the same way as moving from one perfectly good house to another. Not a thing wrong with that house, we just find somewhere else we want to live. Sometimes we change jobs or locations, or sometimes we even change husbands or change wives—things just change as we go through life.

Out of that change comes a good business that is for sale.

Buyers, on the other hand, are normally looking for a way to provide for themselves and their families. Most folks are "buying themselves a job" when they buy a business. I also believe that the word *entrepreneur* is greatly overused in America today. Most folks in our market are not true entrepreneurs or risk takers: they have been pushed into it by circumstances. They are "forced entrepreneurs" who have been downsized, reengineered, rightsized, offshored, or they have a job they do not like, or one that they feel may not offer future job security.

When I first came into this business in 1982, there were only about 3 to 5 percent of folks who said, "I always wanted to be in business for myself." Owning your own business has been called the American Dream, but I am not so sure most folks think that. I think most people would still like a $70,000 or $80,000 or $90,000, or $100,000 per year job that they liked, felt appreciated in, and provided them with job security. I still feel that only 3 to 5 percent have always wanted to be in business for themselves, but I believe that 50 to 60 percent now consider owning their own business as one of their best options to provide for themselves, given the present world of work and lack of job security.

The government statistics are way off—as always, statistics can be used to show anything. The government says that unemployment is down (5 to 6 percent). What they don't count is how many folks are "underemployed," not unemployed. We are not talking about people who are in the unemployment line but about those who are doing something to provide some sort of income. They are consultants, part-time employees, or freelancers, just doing something to pay the bills while searching for work. There are very few high-paying jobs out there for laid-off executives, and there are very few jobs for folks over 40—and who isn't over 40? And anyone over 40 is eminently overqualified for an entry-level job.

It used to be that when you sent out 10 résumés, you would get several job interviews and probably several job offers. Today, you send out 100 résumés and no one calls you back, especially if you're past the magic age. The main reason they won't give you the job is that they know you are not going to take a $30,000 per year position and stay there. You'll only take the job for immediate income and spend all your time trying to get a better job, while in contrast a young person right out of school will consider a $30,000 job great when compared to their current salary of nothing. With a

$30,000 salary, they can afford their own apartment and some wheels.

Job interviewers ask anyone north of 40, "Do you understand computers?" and we say, "Oh, sure. I can run Windows." The kid right out of college can write code, for goodness sakes; he can build computers! He's been raised on computers and video games. Who do you think the company is going to hire?

I'm in the same boat. No one is going to give me a $30,000 per year job, because I cannot possibly live on that salary what with three daughters, two stepdaughters, two ex-wives, and two husbands-in-law. I am probably better off providing an income and job security by owning my own business. So are you!

5

Finding the Right Business for You

Success Isn't Easy

For those looking for a job or a business to provide for themselves and their families, I think the most important thing to do is to *find a business that you like!* I do not mean that if you like to go fishing you've got to get into the fishing business, but it's tough to put the necessary energy into something you don't like. If you hate to get up and go to work each day, then you've got a problem. I don't care how smart you are or what kind of business it is.

If folks are still having trouble deciding in which direction to head, I ask them to think back to their childhood, from ages seven to fifteen. What did you like to spend your time doing when you were completely free to do whatever it was that you wanted to do? You used and developed your talents in that period of your life as freely as you wished. You may now look at becoming the owner of your own business in the same way—and there are no limits to what you can do or what you can consider.

Another necessity for success in owning a business is a willingness to work smart, hard, long hours. You can forget the 8-hour day and the 40-hour week. Most of the folks I know who are successful in their own business put in 10 to 12 hours per day and 50- to 60-hour workweeks.

For instance, my brother Ben is a successful small businessman: he's a medical doctor, a pediatrician. Let's look at his and his wife Faye's investment in their success. Four years of college, four years of medical school, two years of an internship, two years of residency in his specialty, and then he began his service business. He worked at the hospital to pay his way through medical school, and Faye worked as a teacher. He makes rounds at a hospital beginning at 7 a.m. and then goes to his office. He has some wonderful partners; however, he is on call all night certain evenings and one weekend per month. He works hard and long hours and is successful.

I have heard that professional athletes usually put in 30 hours of practice time for every hour in the game. That is after years of Little League, high school sports, and four years of college sports before they became professionals.

Fortunately, most folks who are successful like what they're doing, and therefore the long, hard hours do not seem so long and hard.

In most things in life, as you climb the mountain of success, if you break the journey down into small steps, you will have a much better chance of succeeding. When I was in the construction business, I learned something interesting. The international height of a step is 7½ inches. You can climb up several flights of stairs at one time, if it is a standard step. Have you ever tried to walk up steps that are a foot high? You'll get exhausted. It works the other way around also. Have you ever experienced a small step stairway, three to four inches? You almost trip because the human body is used to a 7½-inch step. When making a decision, try to break the decision process down into small standard steps. Take life and business decisions one step, one day, at a time.

Getting Started: Think About Your Options

When you look at a book with a title like "How to Buy a Business in America," it usually tells you to first get the financials and take them to a good accountant. If it's a good business, he'll advise you to buy it. I've been in this business for almost 22 years and I've never once, *not once*, had an accountant advise a client to buy a business unless it was a franchise. The accountants have been hired to protect their client, and if they are going to err, they are going to err on the side of caution.

Besides, accountants are only looking at the financials, not the business: the location, product or service, trained employees, furniture, fixtures and equipment, existing customers, cash flow, and the track record. The financials have been prepared with one main focus, and that is to pay no taxes or to minimize taxes. They have not been done to show how well the business is doing. (More about how the financials relate to the value of the business later.)

Second, the book on "How to Buy a Business" tells you to get these financials, do a great business plan, and take them to your friend the banker with whom you play golf every Thursday or know socially. Your banker has already assured you that he'll make you a business loan when you need it; after all, he is vice president of [insert the name of your bank], the small business lender for your city. Yeah, right. He has already assured you that he'll lend you the money—*but he won't*—so don't operate under that impression and let that banker humiliate you on the golf course. Go ahead and beat him—bad. He's not going to lend you the money because he *can't*, for reasons I will explain shortly.

Third, the book instructs you to see a good business attorney. If it's a good business, he'll advise you to buy it; if not, he won't. Remember, he has also been hired to protect you, not to do the deal, and the only way to protect you totally is for you not to do the deal. If you do in fact do the deal, he will want to slant it so strongly to your side that the other side won't agree to the terms.

If you never want to take a chance that you'll have to go through the human pain and agony and heartbreak of a divorce, your attorney can protect you. Just don't get married, or get a prenuptial agreement to protect you. I don't know of a quicker way to kill a romance than to say, "Sweetheart, before we go any further into this relationship, I want you to look over and sign this little agreement my attorney has proposed." Good luck! You won't have to worry about getting divorced because, unless you are Donald Trump, you'll never get married.

Don't get too upset with lawyers, accountants, and bankers, though—just realize that they have been trained to look for problems. They have been hired to protect you, not to help you do the deal and buy the business. However, when you don't buy a business, you still don't have a job or an income, so they have not helped you solve your problem. A business broker's job is to help you find a solution to your problem by helping you find the best business opportunity for you.

The most important thing is to keep the focus on the business and to find a business that you like and feel you can manage. Normally you are much better off finding an existing business or a franchise than you are starting up a business, for several reasons. The existing business or a franchise has an established track record; the very fact that it has *survived*

in the marketplace for three years or longer has a major impact on value.

There are advantages to buying an existing business, according to my friend, Tom West, former president, executive director, and founder of the International Business Brokers Association (IBBA) and *the* Acknowledged Guru of Business Brokerage.

An existing business has

1. Actual, rather than pro forma, results
2. Immediate cash flow
3. Trained employees in place
4. Established suppliers and credit
5. Established customers and referral business
6. Existing licenses and permits
7. Training by the seller
8. The availability of owner financing, and this caveat: the success or failure of the business is the owner's responsibility and there is no "right" or perfect business, so buyers must be flexible

It Takes Time to Find and Grow a Business

When I first bought the other folks out of Sunbelt, in the mid-1980s, we had an office in Charleston and one on Hilton Head Island. I learned quickly that I could not successfully run an office that was two and a half hours away. This is a relationship building business, and relationships take time to build. Every time I would drive down to Hilton Head to meet with a buyer and/or seller, we would have a very good one- or two-hour meeting; however, nothing ever came of it.

Also, every time I'd leave Charleston to drive to Hilton Head, I'd drive past 5,000 businesses and waste a day. I learned two things through owning the office in Hilton Head: (1) I reproved the adage that I'd have a much better chance of helping a person who wants or needs a business than one who has lots of money and doesn't really want or need a business; and (2) Hilton Head is a strange and beautiful place—everyone there is a multimillionaire, and you can't raise $10,000 *cash* on the whole damn island! I closed that office—it was not working for me.

In 1986, by happenstance or divine intervention, I met and fell in love with my present and *last* wife, Elaine. The year preceding our wedding, I had built our brokerage staff in Charleston to 14 agents. I determined that was too many, forcing me to spend all my time managing brokers when I like doing deals myself. So I got down to just myself and one other broker, and that was too few. We could not possibly handle the volume of business, and certainly could not dominate our market with only two brokers.

As a side note, during that pared-down time in 1985 a very telling thing happened. I was attending the birthday party of a friend, Peggy Hendricks, and during the normal chitchat and pleasantries of seeing old friends socially, I ran into a young lady whom I had known for years. She was a bright and charming daughter of a prominent businessman who owned the Budweiser distributorship for lower South Carolina, Pearlstine Distributors. She had married a nice young man from California, who had soon learned one of the absolute "rules of nature": if you marry a girl from Charleston, you're going to end up having to move to Charleston. When I welcomed the groom to Charleston, his bride introduced me as Ed Pendarvis, owner of Sunbelt Busi-

ness Brokers, and added, *"They're huge!"* I'm thinking to myself, Huge? Just me and one other fellow and one small office in Charleston? However, I found out she was on to something that has helped us grow.

Folks like the name "Sunbelt" and feel that they have heard of Sunbelt in a positive way. The "Sunbelt," a wonderful section of the country, a Sunbelt Coca-Cola Distributor, a Sunbelt Construction Company, a Sunbelt Trucking Company, a Sunbelt Rentals Company, etc. What's in a name? A great deal, thank you, and thanks to Susan Pearlstine for making me aware of that.

From 1986 to 1989, I tried different ways to grow. I bought a small corner grocery/convenience store with my brother-in-law, George, and he did very well there for a year or so. Then I made a mistake and pushed him to buy another store two blocks away. Again I proved to myself what I learned in Hilton Head: you can run one business, but running two is not easy. After some frustrating times, we decided to sell the stores. George can fix anything, so he went into the construction business, and I decided to stick with business brokerage. Fortunately, since we were business brokers, we were able to sell both stores for a profit. And George opened George Bowen Repairs and helps a lot of folks in his service business.

Another time, I decided to buy a small manufacturing company, Charleston Chimes, from a wonderful lady named Peggy Leland. She had developed a good product and a respected name in the local tourist market. Charleston has a thriving tourist industry, with approximately 4 million visitors per year. The chimes were tuned to the Charleston church bells, and she made them in a small house behind her house on James Island with the help of a neighbor lady. She had built up a 20-store local customer base, including my wife's shop, Elaine's in the Market. At Sunbelt, many buyers were looking for a manufacturing company; however, they were looking for a much larger business than Charleston Chimes.

So I bought the company, built a shed behind our home, and went into the wind chime manufacturing and distributing business. We even took the product to the Atlanta Gift Mart for a couple of years. However, finding myself working until 2 or 3 a.m. making wind chimes, I proved again that there are only 24 hours in each day. I could not make wind chimes all night and broker business deals all day. I decided to sell the wind chime business before I cut one of my thumbs off cutting out the metal pieces.

Charleston has always been a wonderful artists' community. In 1992, I purchased the rights to all prints done by one of the city's favorite artists, Ed Emerson. I first met Mr. Emerson when I built him a condo at Snee Farms. He was a retired Navy chaplain, and he began his art career at our development. When he decided to retire, he came to Sunbelt to sell his line of prints. So Elaine and I bought it.

I also started a small greeting card company, called "Your House Greetings," through Elaine's shop. In the construction business, I used to draw up my own plans, and I liked drawing houses. Now, folks could send me a picture of their house and I would draw a pen and ink sketch of it on a note card and run them off at Kinko's. However, I found I could not draw enough of them to make a living, so I decided to stick with selling businesses.

In 1989, I sold a string of One Hour Martinizing dry cleaning plants and a "drop off" station to Dennis D'Annunzio, an accountant/businessman who was moving to Charleston from Charlotte, North Carolina, with his family. He was and is a good, smart, experienced businessman, and he did adequate due diligence on his purchase. What he didn't realize, however, is how hot it gets in Charleston in the summer, and being from Detroit originally, he found out the hard way that he hated the dry cleaning business.

He said he found out that if the "presser" or "spotter" doesn't show up, guess who's back there pressing and spotting in the 120 degree heat? The owner, CPA, president/CEO, or whoever else is in charge. Dennis says: "I'm not too worried about dying and going to hell. I've already been there."

Since he hated the business, consequently he did not do well in it, and in 1991 he came back to our office. At Sunbelt we sell businesses to you and can sell them for you. We resold the dry cleaning businesses, and the folks who bought them are still doing well. One Hour Martinizing is a good business; it just was not a good business for Dennis.

Dennis was looking for something else to do, and I suggested that he come and work with me at Sunbelt Business Brokers. It was one of the best business decisions I've made. Fortunately for me, he agreed and utilized his deal-making talents—unusual for a CPA—to be a very successful broker. Often, CPAs can only focus on the numbers; Dennis can focus on the people, the business, the product, and the deal as well. And I realized that two horses can pull a wagon faster, farther, easier, and quicker than one.

A few months later I invited him to breakfast at Nathan's Deli and suggested that he come into Sunbelt Business Brokers as an equity partner with me. I thought that we could grow the company together, because the need for this type of business service was so great. I told him that I felt we had something to sell, but that neither of us could take a salary initially, because the company could not afford it. We would have to live on our personal commissions; however, if he joined me, I'd make him a millionaire.

Dennis is a smart, hardworking, determined businessman, and we complement each other. In 2000, at Sunbelt's annual meeting in Charleston, I asked him to serve as CEO, handling all operations for the company as we continued our growth. The following year I asked him to serve as president and CEO. Also around this time, we were fortunate to add another strong broker, Tom Conroy, to the Charleston Sunbelt office. This allowed Dennis and me to focus our efforts on growing the Sunbelt franchise.

In June 1991 we opened an office in Greenville, South Carolina, and within 90 days we had the best and largest business brokerage firm in Greenville, even though there were five other existing business brokers there when we started.

We did the same thing in Columbia and Myrtle Beach, South Carolina; Charlotte, North Carolina; Augusta and Savannah, Georgia. In 1993 we filed our franchise documents. We got our Federal Trademark Registration and began franchising in earnest. We have truly been blessed, and have been growing at a steady 30 percent per year. We now have over 350 offices in 47 states and 11 foreign countries.

In the January 1995 issue of *Entrepreneur* magazine, Sunbelt was rated the number one business brokerage franchise in America in their annual listing of the Top 500 franchises. We repeated that designation for the ensuing five years and in the 2003 and 2004 issues. We made the Top 100 fastest growing franchises, normally sustaining our growth at a rate of 30 percent per year.

In 1995, Sunbelt had 35 offices; in 1996, 65; 1997, 97; 1998, 132; 1999, 178; and by the year 2000, we had 218 offices in 40 states and 8 foreign countries.

When Dennis and I first put together our franchise program, we did two things considerably different from other franchisors. First we decided to have a "flat fee" for a franchise, rather than a percentage or royalty that would have been based on a percentage of gross sales of our franchises. The idea was that when someone became very successful, they would have the incentive to *stay* with Sunbelt Business Brokers, not *drop out* because the percentage royalty became too much money to part with. Second, we decided that to help our offices be successful, we had to put a great deal of emphasis on training, and train not just the office owners, but all the individual brokers as well. I am president of the company, and now chairman, but I have personally trained every broker and agent, one on one, over the last 12 years. That has proven to be a good idea and has afforded me the wonderful opportunity to meet every broker in every office.

My friend Bill Law in Charlotte, North Carolina, our fourth Sunbelt office, has been very successful, normally doing well over $1 million per year in commission income. If Bill had to send us $60,000 or $80,000 in royalty payments, he probably would have dropped out of the Sunbelt network long ago. His fee is constant and is an incentive to stay with Sunbelt rather than drop out. I haven't trained a broker in Charlotte in over four years. He has a stable and professional group of eight brokers who have been with him for years. However, we probably trained over 30 brokers in Charlotte before he settled on his core professional group.

Bill is an important fixture on the Sunbelt team who has been good for us, and we applaud his success. We also decided that we would have to train all the broker/agents because business brokerage is a very different and difficult business discipline and very few folks know how to do it. So we set up a training program where we hold a two-day "basic business broker training class" every week. We started our training in Columbia, South Carolina, once a month, for the offices in Columbia, Greenville, Spartanburg, Myrtle Beach, Charleston, Charlotte, Augusta, and Savannah. As our office network grew, we moved training to Charlotte, Atlanta, and Orlando every month. Then to Washington, D.C., then Los Angeles, Dallas, and so on.

Sunbelt Business Brokers also had no national advertising fee, since we believe the local office knows best how to spend the precious advertising dollars in their market. We recommend $250 to $500 per month in the yellow pages and $1,500 per month in the largest local Sunday newspaper. We advertise in the "Business Opportunity" or "Business for Sale" section. Now, we do have a national advertising fee that each office pays to grow the brand awareness of Sunbelt, and the Internet is where we do the most advertising.

Also, we decided to invite *prospective* brokers and franchisees to our training without cost or obligation. At first everyone we talked to said that was not a good idea; however, we felt that since this was such a different business from what people think it is, we'd rather spend two days with someone—get to know them a bit and get them to know us and the Sunbelt system—before we sign an agreement and become partners. A franchise, by definition, is a partnership whereby we license someone the use of the Sunbelt name and system of business brokerage, which we feel works. Out of our mutual success they pay us a flat amount every month as a fixed royalty. This royalty never goes up. This concept has allowed us to build a strong platform of impressive franchise partners who have led Sunbelt to success worldwide. Many of our franchisees make a lot of money.

This business attracts executive-type, independent, self-confident people, and we've got some real superstars. It is also a testament to our franchise operation that we have never once had a lawsuit with one of our franchisees.

We felt, and still feel, that the main obligation of training is to get a broker to understand and believe in the value of small business. His or her success depends on understanding small business, the sellers and the buyers, and also a proven Sunbelt system of how to help them get to where they want to go. I call it the buyer's and seller's *Goal Line*. I also figure that I've got about 90 days to help a new broker make some money as a broker, or his wife will make him get a "real job." So I try to get a new broker up and running as quickly as possible.

The Importance of Relationships

Doing all of the initial training of brokers for Sunbelt has proven very helpful to me because I know personally who is on the other end of the telephone when one of them calls, and so do the brokers I've trained. Those two days together help us build a relationship. In this business, as in life in general, relationships are everything. And it gives us the opportunity to share ideas about the basic approaches to this business and the strategies that help our brokers better serve our clients and customers.

In a real estate deal, there is no "real" relationship between the seller and the buyer; in fact, most folks don't even know who owned the house they live in now, before they bought it, or whom they sold their last house to. Most often the buyer and seller don't even meet each other until what I call a one-hour "happy talk" meeting at closing. Usually the closing in a real estate deal is the beginning and end of a brief relationship between the seller and the buyer. It's the alpha and the omega of the relationship and transaction. What a different world from business brokerage!

In a business deal the closing is the *beginning* of the relationship—especially if the seller finances a part of the sale price for 5, 7, or 10 years. Since the seller is going to finance at least part of the sale, a substantial portion of his or her money is invested in the continued success of the business *after the sale*. If you buy a franchise, the closing *begins* the relationship between the franchisor and the franchisee.

Remember that in business, relationships are everything. It is the relationship, both personal and financial, that makes the deals work. The main focus of our business has always been on listing businesses to sell when an owner wants or needs to sell, and helping a buyer find a business to buy when he wants or needs to buy; working with both parties to arrive at a price, terms, and conditions that work for all parties; a level playing field; a win-win relationship.

Business brokerage is different from any business that I have ever been in. You have to build an honest relationship between the seller and the broker, between the buyer and the broker, and between the seller and the buyer. Unlike real estate, where you normally have a broker dealing with the seller and another broker dealing with the buyer, in most business sales the Sunbelt broker is the only broker involved in the transaction. I like that for two reasons: (1) we have to be sensitive and responsive to both the buyer and the seller, and (2) there are very few commission splits, so we get a $1 dollar, not a "50-cents dollar."

In the next chapter we'll look at the real value a business broker brings to the marketplace.

6

The Real Purpose and Value of a Business

WHAT'S THE REAL PURPOSE of a business? Some folks would say the purpose of a business is to make a profit. Some would say it's to get and keep customers for your product and/or service. Others would say it's to be a viable economic force that provides a product and/or service. I think the real purpose of a business is to provide a living or an income for the owner and his or her family.

What do you want or need out of a job? I assume it is the same thing: to provide a living or an income. Now, hopefully the business or job will also be rewarding in other ways: challenging, interesting, growth opportunities, etc. However, first and foremost it must offer a sufficient financial reward.

So ultimately the question is: Do I take this job? Do I start this business? Do I buy this business? You can work for someone else or you can work for yourself. In either case what you need from that job or that business is the same. If I take this job, if I "buy" this job, if I buy this business, how much money will I make, and will I have the opportunity to grow from there, income and otherwise?

Well, to get the answers to these very important questions so we can make the best decision, we have to define our territories, borders, or boundaries, so we are on the same sheet of music.

Making the Decision to Buy a Business

Almost all decisions that we make in life are products of and framed by the following:

- A subconscious process of elimination: When you bought your house or car, did you not have a lot of options to choose from? When you chose your wife or husband, did you not eliminate the entire rest of the world? When you eat out and choose your food from a menu, don't you eliminate all the other choices?
- Making the best decision with "all things considered." In other words, based on where we are in our work and family lives, with all things considered, we need to make the best decision we can about how to provide for our families. With job security gone, maybe buying a business is the best solution.

In making this decision, let's look at the world of business as seen today in America.

Everything we study in school about business, every subject we take in formal education in America, especially in college and postgraduate study, is about *big business*, publicly traded companies and giant private companies. All we see and hear from the talking heads on TV is about big business. Everything we read in the newspaper is about big business news.

What happened today on the New York Stock Exchange? What happened on the Nasdaq? What happened in the S&P Index, etc.? When you realize that all we study in school and see in the media is about big business, it explains our understanding and interpretation of business rules and definitions, all pertaining to big business (mostly publicly traded companies).

No one graduates from college, gets a diploma, and knows one thing about running a convenience store, dry cleaning plant, auto repair business, or restaurant. They know a lot about running IBM, General Motors, Coca-Cola, or Microsoft, but very little about the real world of small business.

Isn't that strange, when you realize that approximately 98 percent of businesses in America are small businesses? Our entire educational plant in America is geared toward one thing: get a job, and work for someone else in big business.

The Small Business Administration (SBA), our government, defines a very small business as one that generates less than $20 million in gross sales per year or has 100 employees or less. Isn't that weird? In the "real world" of small business that's a *huge* business. The government doesn't seem to know that we exist, and that is probably good, not bad. They even quit trying to keep records and statistics on small business in 1996.

You have to understand that everything is relative. The government calls General Motors, Exxon-Mobil, Wal-Mart, AOL, and Microsoft big business. A medium-sized business would be one that generates from $100 million to $500 million in annual gross sales. Under $100 million down to $20 million is a smaller-sized business, and under $20 million is a very small business.

Of all businesses in America, 95 percent do $1 million or less in annual gross sales and have 20 employees or less. Another 3 percent do $30 million or less and have 100 employees or less. The government and our colleges and universities do not notice that small business exists, and yet very small businesses have provided 80 percent of the jobs and family incomes that big businesses have been shedding for the last 12 years.

Here is an example: Let's say I own a convenience store along the road on the way home in any big or small city. One fellow stops in to pay for his gas and some convenience items and he says, "Ed, can you believe what happened in the stock market today? The Dow dropped 282 points!"

I say, "Wow! Isn't that unbelievable? That will be $28.17, Mr. Jones."

The next person in line says, "Did you see what happened today in Russia [Afghanistan, China, India, South America . . .]?"

I say, "I'll tell you, Mr. Johnson, you never know. It's always something, isn't it? That will be $17.23."

The next lady says, "Ed, can you believe what the school board, the Federal Reserve Board, the president, or the Democrats are doing? It's terrible."

I say, "Yes, ma'am, it's always something. That will be $19.88."

At the end of the day, at the end of the week, at the end of the month, no matter what happens in the world, I have made enough money to pay all of my business expenses, my house payment, my car payment, and I have fed my children.

America's Amazing Economic Engine

Small business, sometimes referred to as "mom-and-pop" businesses, is "America's Amazing Economic Engine," and it runs right along through the ups and downs of the stock market. It runs right along through the ups and downs of interest rates. It runs no matter who the president is or what Congress does and no matter what's happening in China, the

Middle East, at the Federal Reserve, or on the world stage. Small business is the stabilizing force that does exactly what it is supposed to do, which is to provide a living for the owner and his or her family, and it provides all the jobs that the big companies have eliminated. It is the real economy. It is indeed "America's Amazing Economic Engine!"

Now small business differs from big business in some major ways, so for the purposes of getting on the same wavelength, please let me share with you some of the things I share with all of my business brokers in training.

The Differences between Big and Small Business

You see, when I do the new broker training sessions for Sunbelt Business Brokers, I feel that the most important part of training is to help our brokers see the real value of a small business. Because they are just like the rest of us, they have come out of a background and educational plant that only understands and promotes big business.

Three major differences in big business and small business as they relate to the real world are found in the areas of financials, management, and what I call the size of the commitment. Also, it helps to realize that what we call big businesses are normally "publicly traded" companies: stock market companies that sell shares of stock or equity in the corporation to the public as well as to large investors, such as banks, college investment groups, retirement programs, union benefits, insurance companies, mutual funds, other corporations, etc. They may have thousands or even millions of "owners" or stockholders.

Big businesses have "audited" financial statements, and they have to comply with Generally Accepted Accounting

Practices (GAAP), as set by accounting regulations. The financials have to be current, correct, complete, and audited by an unbiased CPA firm (unbiased except that they would like to keep the company's business, of course, as in Arthur Andersen and the Enron Corporation scandal).

Financials

First, let's look at the financials. Have you ever heard the axiom that a business has two sets of books? One set for management purposes and another set of books for the IRS? Well, it's absolutely true! *Big business* has two sets of books, while small business usually only has one set of books that aren't too accurate, current, or complete. In big business, one set of books is for public consumption, with a nice glossy print prospectus that is sent to you when you purchase stocks. For instance, when you buy stocks in General Motors, IBM, Coca-Cola, Microsoft, or McDonald's, they send you a nice overview of the company with recast financial statements, complete with notes to the balance sheets and income statements, and a nice optimistic report from the president of the company or the chairman of the board. Great prospectus! Buy our stock!

Now let me ask you something. Have you ever seen the tax return for General Motors? For IBM, Coca-Cola, or McDonald's? Absolutely not, and you never will. That information is compiled on the other side of the accounting house, with all the smart CPAs and tax lawyers doing everything they possibly can to "legally" take advantage of the tax laws and tax codes to help their clients pay no taxes or the minimum amount of taxes.

You would not believe how much money General Motors "loses" for tax purposes. General Electric from 1981 to 1984 not only paid no taxes on over $6.2 billion in pretax profits, but they got back $273 million they had already paid in taxes (remember the net operating loss scenario). There is nothing legally wrong with this practice no matter how wrong it seems. The big business companies take advantage of all of the tax laws that their lobbyists have gotten Congress to write to protect the "cash flow" of the company, to build and grow the company, and to enhance shareholder value. Over 60 percent of large corporations paid no taxes on profits in 2003.

Small business doesn't have the luxury of having two sets of books. They do not need and cannot afford a glossy print prospectus for public stockholders; they are a "private business" and no one sees their books. So they only have one set of books, which are usually not very accurate, complete, or current. However, just like the big companies' second set of books that the public doesn't see, the books of a small business are done to take advantage of the tax laws and tax codes, to help these companies pay no taxes or to at least minimize taxes. The books are done to *minimize* taxes and *maximize* the owner's lifestyle.

Small business owners also attempt to protect the "cash flow" of the company, to provide for the needs of the business, to grow the business, and to enhance shareholder (owner) value. They teach you in school that the purpose of the business is to make a profit, right? No, profit is a bad word when it comes to taxes. You have to pay taxes on profits.

Your business can do $300,000 in annual gross sales or $3 million or $30 million in gross sales; if at the end of the year the business shows no profits for tax purposes, no taxes are due. In fact, if a business shows a loss for tax purposes, you may use that to shelter future profits or perhaps get back taxes you paid the last three years on prior profits. When a big company announces a layoff of thousands of workers, a restructuring charge is taken, and they write it off.

Now please understand this is a very important part of the real world of business, especially the world of small business. You can go for *years* without a profit, but you cannot go a *week* without cash flow. A business will not survive for long without cash flow or earnings, even though for tax purposes it tries not to ever show a profit.

Management

A second area of differentiation between a big business and a small business is in the management. The president of General Motors, for instance, sits in his corner office on the twenty-second floor of the General Motors office building, which I assume is in Detroit. Well, he has to have correct, accurate, complete, and current financial data to help him manage the company. He could not possibly walk through every manufacturing facility, every sales office or showroom, every financial department, parts department, and service facility, much less the R&D department, and keep up with the leasing programs and advertising programs without current, accurate, complete, and correct financial data.

The small business owner (Mom and Pop) opens the store (restaurant, dry cleaners, auto repair, etc.) at 7 a.m., and is there working in the business, dealing with employees, customers, vendors, equipment, inventory, stocking, production, and sales all day long. These owners do not use financial data to run their business because they are too busy "running" the business.

In fact, after running the business from 7 a.m. to 7 p.m., the last thing in the world they want to do is stay there another hour and make sure that the books balance. Mom and Pop need to go home and take care of themselves and the kids because they have to be back at the store again tomorrow morning at 7 a.m.

Small business owners don't use financial data to manage their business; they manage it by being there, and they normally use what I call "checkbook accounting." They know how much money they have in the bank; they know what the payroll is on Friday; they know the approximate amount of accounts receivable and accounts payable; they know the usual level of inventory; they know when the rent is due; and they know how much business they did last March, April, and May. Their operating "books" are primarily their checkbook.

Mom and Pop use their total knowledge of the business to manage their business, and the accounting function (the books) is almost always in a catch-up mode. Sometimes I'll ask a small business owner for their books and records for this year and they'll say they are working on them. Heck, they don't even have last year's books yet, because they still owe their accountant for 2002. Accountants sometimes have to live with 12-month receivables; however, they know you have to come back to file next year's taxes. They will eventually get paid, God bless them. And when the small business owners do finally get the "shoebox" financials to their accountant, they are usually only interested in one thing: do we have to pay any taxes? Then the annual financials go into a folder, never to be seen again unless or until the owners sell the business.

Folks in California think they're the ones who come up with all these new sayings and expressions. They believe they came up with the phrase "walking around management." Shoot, Mom and Pop have been using "walking around management" and "checkbook accounting" ever since they've been in business. It obviously works.

Size of the Commitment

The third area of differentiation between big business and small business is found in what I call the "size of the commitment in investment." When you buy stock in a big business, it's usually with extra money or savings that you do not use for living expenses. This money is after the basic expenses of house payments, car payments, education, and eating three times a day. It could be spent, put in savings, or invested in stocks or bonds. There is no doubt that the discipline to put away that extra money in investment is important.

However, compare the size of that decision to putting practically all of your life savings into the down payment on a business purchase or start-up, and add to that the additional commitment of getting up every morning for the rest of your known life, at least six days per week, and going to work for eight, ten, twelve hours per day.

Most investor "gurus" would advise you not to have more than 10 percent of your family's net worth in a single investment. Yet most small business owners have 80 to 90 percent of their net worth in their business. It *is* their portfolio.

Look at the difference in the size of the commitment. One is a somewhat passive investment that could be stopped if you chose to, and the other is virtually a total commitment by you and your family. Also, there is one other major difference between big and small business that must be understood to arrive at the real value of small business. There was a period from about 1996 to 2000 when everyone seemed to get stock market fever. The normal returns on investment of making 2 to 3 percent per year in a bank savings account secured by the FDIC, and perhaps doubling that in the risk of the equity or stock market, gave way to "exuberance" in the stock market as folks begin making at least 20 percent return and more in stocks.

Some new IPOs (Initial Public Offerings) on new technology companies that no one had ever heard of became overnight successes. Stock prices shot up hundreds of percentage points, even though these companies didn't have a product or service defined by the real world market yet. The "old rules" of the economy just didn't apply, said some.

Folks signed on to these companies as investors bid up the stocks, and many made fortunes. (*If* you sold the stock at the right time.) Folks quit worrying about their jobs and became "day traders" and stock market "gurus." Investment groups sprung up in neighborhoods.

The day traders, stockbrokers, and employees with stock options; the dreamers and the computer geeks who stayed up all night eating pizza and doing "cool" things on their computers; as well as a lot of very successful Wall Street investors, were riding high and kind of laughing at the rest of the world that missed the ride up. Guess what they found out? Old rules *do* apply. A business, big or small, has to make money. It has to have sales, not just "eyeballs" looking at a Web site that does cool things, and it has to take in more money than it costs to run the business or the business will go out of business. It will not survive.

Now, there is "blood all over the floor" in Silicon Valley and in many technology companies and some areas of the stock market. The day traders are all looking for day jobs. Stock options in many areas were not a good option, and the old rules of investment are back. Good, solid, well-run companies that make a product and/or service that the market responds to and that have earnings are a good long-term investment. How does that relate to the value of a small business? Let's take a look.

Small Businesses Have Only One Source of Income

For a business to be successful, it must have a product and/or service that the market responds to by buying that product or service. Sales drives value, and the old and new business rules say that for a company to be successful, it must have more sales, revenue, or income than it has in the total cost of production and delivery of those products and/or services. In a small business there is usually only one source of income: the sales of the business's product and/or services.

Now in a stock market company or a publicly traded company, there are two major sources of income: (1) sales of the company's product and/or service, and (2) the sale of the company's stock or equity. So the business model is different from a private company, and it is a huge difference.

One of the main advantages of "going public" is the sale of the company's stock, in addition to the sale of its product or service, which can raise tons of "new" money to help a company grow. However, at some point the old rules that say the company has to take in more revenue in sales than it costs to produce those sales comes into play, or they start burning right through the money they received from the sale of their stock.

In the last six months of 1999 and into 2000 the operative word on Wall Street was the "burn rate." How fast will a company "burn" through its IPO cash before it makes more on the sale of its product or service than it costs to operate, which is when it crashes and burns. And the burn rate can go backward too. All through the food chain of investors, big and small, we learned once again that the stock market could go down as well as go up. For some companies, however, where the marketplace did not respond to its product or service, it was and is not coming back up.

Webvan is a great example. The online grocery home delivery announced it was ceasing operations, laying off its last employees, and closing up shop after burning through $835 million. Wow! One thing a lot of technology companies forgot is that Americans like to shop—we don't hate to shop. There are a lot of products that we go to the store to buy; and remember, the retailer brought the stores and their products to our neighborhoods for our shopping convenience.

Again, compare that to small business: a restaurant, dry cleaners, auto repair, or retail business, whose burn rate is immediate. They do not have the luxury of tons of investment money through stock sale or investor money. They have to take in more money every week, every month, and every year than it costs them to operate their business or they will go out of business.

Therefore, the very fact that they have been in business for three, seven, twelve years or longer, tells me beyond a shadow of a doubt that they are taking in more money than it costs to operate their business; otherwise they would have never survived. They not only took in more money than it cost to operate the business, they took in enough extra money so they could also pay their house payment, car payments, feed and educate their children, and perhaps even take a vacation and maybe even invest in savings or the stock market (hopefully not Webvan).

The one thing I know for sure is that if the small business were not paying the owner's bills, he or she would go out of business. As mentioned before, the laws of economics are brutal, disregarding how smart you are, where you went to college, your race, creed, national origin, and who your daddy was. And the laws of economics always apply.

Baseball Rules

Let's use a sports analogy to help define the difference between big business rules, small business rules, and real estate rules. I call big business rules "football rules," small business rules "baseball rules," and real estate rules "basketball rules." Now, all three are ball games, each has a team of players and play in an arena; however, it sure is a different set of rules for each game.

If you tried to play a baseball game in a basketball arena, every time someone hit the ball it would go up in the stands— home run! Everyone would be a Mark McGuire or a Sammy Sosa. In fact the game would get boring after the score got up to 176 to 157 or so.

And if you tried to dribble a basketball on a football field or on a baseball field, it would obviously not work. You see what I mean: you simply have to use the right set of rules for the right ball game.

Most buyers, particularly if they are well-educated college graduates, have a postgraduate degree, or have had work experience in big business, know chapter and verse about big business (football) rules and real estate (basketball) rules, but they do not know anything about small business (baseball) rules.

Often someone comes into my office who has a wonderful and extensive business background, was vice president of this or that Fortune 500 company, has a résumé that will knock your socks off, and has a master's degree in business. Well, he knows a great deal about football rules, but he doesn't know beans about small business (baseball) rules. The problem is he doesn't know that he doesn't know, and so I have to take some time and educate him about baseball rules.

Now if someone comes into my office who has *two* master's degrees, that means he knows "twice as much about nothing." I usually have to put on an extra pot of coffee for this guy because it is going to take a while to reeducate him about baseball rules.

So for the purpose of our discussions about business and business value from now on we will not use real large businesses or publicly traded businesses. We will describe small business, that is, those doing $1 million or less in gross sales annually and that have 20 or less employees. We will describe big business as those doing $1 million to $30 million in gross sales per year, privately held, and that have 100 employees or less. We'll use baseball rules.

7

Business Brokerage Is Not Real Estate Brokerage

WE SAW HOW FOOTBALL rules differ from baseball rules; now let's look at how baseball rules (small business) differ from basketball rules (real estate). Often, folks will assume that since business brokers list and sell other people's assets or property, they are just like real estate brokers. Well, as the Hertz Car Rental ad says, "Not exactly." The two professions differ greatly in application. Yes, the business broker lists and sells things; however, the similarity of the two professions pretty much ends right there.

Baseball rules differ from basketball rules in seven major ways:

1. Confidentiality
2. Financing
3. Relationships
4. Valuation
5. Agency
6. Negotiations
7. Location, location, location

Let's explore each of these differences.

Confidentiality

In a real estate listing, you want to put a sign in the yard; post the property in multiple listings, on the Internet, and elsewhere; and put specific information in real estate publications given away at convenience stores and other locations. You want *everyone* to know that a house or other real estate is for sale.

In small business listings, there is a 180 degree difference. You do not want *anyone* to know that the business is for sale. Not the employees, not the customers, not the competition, nor the vendors, landlords, and banks. It is none of their business that the business is for sale until it becomes their business with a pending sale of the business.

Financing

In the sale of a home, there are hundreds of mortgage companies that will lend you at least 90 percent of the appraised value of the real estate, and if every house in a subdivision sells from a range of $160,000 to $195,000, I can pretty well tell you what a 3-bedroom, 2½-bath house, with a 1-car garage will sell for based on comparable sales in that area. That 90 percent financing helps to develop market value. The fact that so many lenders are willing to give homeowners a 90 percent loan to value (or more) underpins and upholds the value of the house.

Financing a business is again 180 degrees different. Banks do not make small business "acquisition" loans. They say they do, but they don't. Now, they'll lend you money once you own the business and have a proven track record of success—to buy equipment, to buy inventory—or they will make you a small loan to buy a delivery truck. They already have your bank records that show you manage the business successfully, and they see your monthly bank balance (cash flow). But they will not lend you several hundred thousand dollars to *buy* a business. There are two reasons for this.

First, banks don't have any real security in a business loan. With the home loan, if every house in the subdivision sells from $160,000 to $195,000, and if after landing the loan you take off for whatever reason—move to California, get hit by a truck—and do not pay, the bank can foreclose and resell the house for the loan balance, and the mortgage security would pay the loan. A house does not require management the way an operating business does. It could sit empty for several months and probably still sell for from $160,000 to $195,000.

Also, the bank's loss ratio experience in residential home loans in the United States is so low (under 6 percent) that they can actually "bundle" home loan mortgages and sell them in what is called the "secondary market," such as Fannie Mae or Freddie Mac. That way they do not have their money tied up in the loan.

In contrast, a business requires management. If the bank were to make you a business loan and you take off or get hit by a truck, how would the bank get its money back? They cannot operate the business. If they foreclose and close the doors on an operating business, the hard asset value of the business goes down to practically nothing. For instance, if you had a dry cleaner or a restaurant with $300,000 worth of equipment and you close the doors, the value of the equipment goes to maybe 10 cents on the dollar. You'll be lucky if you can give the equipment away. There is another problem. The rent is due, and landlords and other creditors may have dibs on the assets.

Every now and then the banks look at the size of the small business market and say, "We have got to get into that market." However, small business lending has proven to be a very difficult arena for banks, even with SBA guarantees.

For five years running, the most aggressive small business lender in America was the Money Store based in Sacramento, California. In 1998, First Union Bank bought the Money Store; in 2000 they shut down the Money Store, laid off 3,000 employees overnight, and wrote off $3 billion in bad loans. They proved once again that when you have to foreclose on a small business loan, "it ain't going to be pretty."

In November 2000 another very aggressive small business lender, Transamerica Small Business Capital, shut down overnight, laid off all of their staff, and got out of the business of small business lending. They were followed by Heller Financial in 2001.

When it comes to small business, banks do not really have any security. If the business model doesn't work, if the business does not produce earnings and a living for the owner, the bank knows it won't get paid. Good credit does not pay the loan payments—cash flow pays the loan payments.

Also, banks are risk averse. They do not want to take a risk that cannot be covered by security under the worst-case scenario. The banks' definition of security in a worst-case scenario is what assets can be seized, taken to market within 30 to 60 days, and sold, so they can get their money back.

Besides, banks usually define small business as those doing from $3 million to $20 million in annual gross sales. So even though the banks take out full-page ads in the newspapers and are on television saying, "We are the small business lenders," they very seldom make small business *acquisition* loans. I would like to suggest that they take some of that advertising money and really make some small business loans!

Since the bank doesn't have any security in a business loan, it will not lend you the money. Unless, of course, you put up some outside security, such as your house, for instance. But your wife is probably too smart for that, and if she doesn't think it's a good idea to put up your house for security to buy a business, she'll probably stop you. And if she can't stop you, she'll call her daddy, and her daddy never really liked you very much anyway. So he says, "Put that boy on the phone right now. He is not putting my little girl and my grandchildren on the street for some crazy business deal! Tell that boy to get a job like I did!"

I don't blame your wife. I wouldn't put my house up for security to buy a business either; it's too much of a risk. A business ought to stand for its own security.

The second reason banks will not finance a business is that they must have proven debt repayment ability. Your friendly banker will always say, "Bring in the last three years financials and tax returns on the business and we're ready to go."

However, if you bring in the tax returns, never stand in front of the banker. He'll probably throw up all over the floor because he's already told you he'd give you a loan and he can't figure out how in the world he's going to get paid back out of the financials. He's got to see enough money in the financials after taxes to repay the bank (which is the bank's main concern) and enough for you to make a living.

Seldom will the financials show that. They have not been prepared to show how well the business is doing, but prepared for one main purpose: to pay no taxes. So banks will not lend you the money because they do not have security and they do not have proven debt repayment ability. Also, there is no reliable secondary funding sources for small business loans, like Fannie Mae or Freddie Mac, to "take out" the bank's investment.

Now, if the bank or another lender can get an SBA guarantee, that would constitute the bank's security. The very fact that a lender will make the loan gives you a certain comfort level, in that they feel the business deal will work. The bank or lender has approved the financials and believes the business will continue to be successful. If they make you a loan and you get hit by a truck, get a divorce, take off for parts unknown, or the business model doesn't work for whatever reason, the bank simply calls the security (SBA) for repayment.

Usually, the SBA guarantee is at an interest rate of prime plus 2.25 to 2.75 percent. So it also costs more. However, with the SBA guarantee, the bank may lend the money. The SBA, however, always requires your house as additional security. They don't like risk either.

In fact, you need the same things in a home loan: security and proven debt repayment. The security is in the property, based on comparable market value, and debt repayment is your employment verification or proven income records.

Seller Financing

For the same two reasons that a *bank* won't make the loan, the *seller* should make you the loan, and the seller is in a far better position to finance the business.

First, security. If for some reason you didn't pay the seller, he could foreclose and take the business back. Whereas the bank would simply close the doors and lose everything because it couldn't manage the business, the seller could step back in and take over management of the business to protect his investment. He doesn't want to, of course, but he could. The seller is in a far more secure position than the bank because he can run the business until he could sell it again.

And second, as far as the financials are concerned, who knows more about the actual cash flow or earnings of the business than the seller, for goodness sake? He or she has been running the business for years and providing for his family out of the business. Forget the financials and tax returns showing a loss, the seller knows better than anyone (and he is the only one who truly knows) whether the earnings of the business can allow for debt repayment to him and still leave enough money for the buyer and his family to live on.

So the very fact that the seller will lend you the money to buy the business—or that he *won't* lend you the money to buy the business—probably tells you more about the value of the business than anything else.

In fact, I personally believe very strongly in seller financing. I call it "the seller putting his money where his mouth is." He says, "I'm selling you a good business that I truly believe will continue to be successful and make you a living, Mr. Buyer, just like it has done for me. Therefore, I am willing to lend you part of the money to buy it."

Also, seller financing is important for this reason: unlike an SBA loan that is prime plus 2.25 to 2.75 percent, seller financing is usually at prime rate or less, not more. The seller knows better than anyone how many dollars you can take out of the cash flow of the business each month to service the debt and still allow the buyer enough money to make a living.

Seller financing is so important to establish the real relationship of buyer to seller in the transaction that I tell my buyers, "If a seller won't finance part of the business sale, I don't believe I'd buy it." You know why I say that? I absolutely *believe* it! The best and only way to be assured that all of the information the seller is telling you about the business is true is for the seller to finance part of the purchase price. Owner financing levels the playing field between the buyer and the seller. It forms a solid bridge in the "leap of faith" between the buyer and seller necessary to put a deal together.

Now, occasionally we have an "all cash" deal. To afford a buyer a comfort level even in an all-cash purchase, we'll get the seller to agree to set aside 20 percent of the purchase price in the closing attorney's escrow account for 60 days after the closing. This allows the buyer to properly transition the business and to verify that the seller's warranties and representations have been accurate.

Relationships

In the real estate business there is no relationship between the buyer and seller. The buyer gets a new mortgage, pays off the old mortgage, and buys the house. Often, the buyer and seller do not even meet, or if they do, it's for that one-hour "happy talk" meeting at the closing.

Small business is 180 degrees different. *Relationships are everything*! The relationship between the business broker and the seller, between the business broker and the buyer, between the buyer and seller.

If the seller is going to finance this sale for 5, 7, or 10 years, there is going to be a 60-, 84-, or 120-month relationship between the buyer and seller. Both parties have a significant vested interest in the continued success of the business. Unlike real estate, where the closing is the beginning and the end of the relationship, in business the closing only *begins* the relationship.

Valuation

What is the value of something? Americans like a definition of value. We normally equate price with value. While shopping in a store, we pick out the items we want, they are run through the scanner at the checkout, and the total is the amount that we pay. In buying a car, we look at the blue book value; in real estate, we look at comparables. At Sunbelt, we often recommend that you get an independent, third-party, certified business appraisal to help you determine market value.

However, when it comes to valuing a business, the financing also plays a major part. As we discussed earlier, if every house in the subdivision sells from $160,000 to $195,000, I can tell you what a house would sell for by figuring that the banks will loan 90-percent-plus of the sales price to a qualified buyer. That financing is a major underpinning of market value.

Think about this: if there were no bank financing, what would a house sell for? Perhaps less, perhaps more. The actual answer is that it would sell for what a ready, willing, and able buyer would and could pay, and what a ready, willing, and able seller would accept. In other words, it would be a true market-value-driven price.

In a business sale, because there is normally no bank financing to underpin the appraised value, a business will sell for what a buyer can and will pay and what a seller will take, given a price and terms and conditions agreeable to everyone. That is the business brokerage market.

Now in this instance, small business value and large business value (publicly traded businesses) are similar. What is a business worth? What the market says it is today; right now, in fact, if the stock exchange is open. You will see all kinds of legitimate approaches to the market value of a business—multiple of earnings, multiples of EBIT (earnings before interest and taxes), and multiples of EBITDA (earnings before interest and taxes, depreciation and amortization). However, the real value is what the stock market says is it right now, determined by what its stock shares are selling for. And just as a lot of day traders and savvy investors found out, the price you paid several months ago might not be the same as the market value today. Check out Lucent Technology and AOL!

Rules of Agency

Business brokers almost always work for the seller. Our legal and fiduciary responsibilities are to the seller. However, we must honestly and fairly deal with the buyer, and we never work against the buyer. A business deal must work for a buyer, or else he or she won't buy, and if the buyer doesn't buy, a seller can't sell. And the market sets the value.

A business deal needs to be a win-win situation for both buyer and seller or it won't work. We don't usually work with a foolish buyer or a foolish seller, nor do I want to deal with them. Also, there is little co-brokering in business brokerage, primarily because of confidentiality issues. The brokerage firm that lists a business usually also sells the business.

Concerning the rules of agency, we disclose our agency relationships to buyers and sellers alike. Both must have confidence in the broker's fairness and honesty, or they will probably not buy or sell. The business broker serves as a "finder" and a "facilitator." The broker does not warrant the correctness, completeness, or accuracy of the information that the seller provides to the buyer about the business: it's up to the buyer to do his or her own due diligence on the business and/or the seller. Likewise, the broker does not warrant the qualifications of the buyer: it's up to the seller to do his or her own due diligence on the buyer. The broker is like a preacher in a marriage ceremony: we perform the service of putting the two together; however, you cannot blame the preacher if the marriage doesn't work—or the broker if the business deal doesn't work. IT IS NOT OUR FAULT!

Negotiations

Americans are generally not comfortable negotiating. We think we are, but we're not. In almost all of our transactions, we equate price with value, and we either pay the price or we don't buy. It is perfectly normal and acceptable to just walk away; however, we have a cultural bias against negotiations.

If you were going through a checkout line at the grocery store or a Wal-Mart, Kmart, Sears, or Home Depot and the bill was $68.20, you wouldn't think of asking, "Would you take $40 cash for these items?" Nice people do not negotiate. If you do not believe that, try to negotiate at the next checkout line with your kids standing next to you. They will slowly move away from you without making eye contact, hoping that no one noticed and realized that you are their daddy.

The only items that "nice people" can negotiate on comfortably are at flea markets, yard sales, or when buying a car. However, every time they take a survey about what folks don't like about buying a car, guess what the number one answer is? The hassle of negotiating.

Now, in buying a business, you have to negotiate. *Well,* you do not *have* to, but here's what I mean. Let's say the seller is asking $200,000 with a $100,000 down payment, and you only have $40,000 in down payment ability. If you were going to buy the business, it would have to be no more than a $40,000 down payment and the seller would have to finance the balance, or else there will be no sale.

There is a major difference with a foreign buyer, however, because foreign buyers have a cultural bias *toward* negotiating. They come from cultures where everything is negotiable. Approximately 20 percent of small business buyers are foreign buyers.

Haven't you noticed how many convenience stores, liquor stores, coin ops, dry cleaners, restaurants, laundries, and motels "new" Americans own? Indian buyers; Asian buyers; Middle Eastern buyers; South American buyers; Russian, Canadian, Mexican, and European buyers: all summarily dismiss the asking price and just make an offer. These new Americans have a strong motivation to buy a business because it is almost politically impossible to get a "work visa" to come to America. The government looks at that as taking jobs away from Americans. However, with an E-2 Visa or an L1 Visa, a "substantial investment visa," politically, the government views that as a way of investing in and adding to the economy, in providing jobs and saving jobs. So for some foreigners, that is the ticket to America. But you can expect strong negotiations on price and terms.

Location, Location, Location

In the real estate business (I have been in the real estate business in South Carolina since 1970), we always say the three most important things that influence value are location, location, and location. Well, in business that is not necessarily true. The three most important things that influence value in a business are:

1. *Location (depending on the type of business).* A restaurant, convenience store, or retail business's success may depend heavily on its location. A janitorial business or lawn care business could be located in a garage somewhere, and location may have little to do with its value.

2. *Track record.* The very fact that the business has survived for three years or longer and has an established customer base, an existing cash flow, trained employees, a trend of sales, and a product or service that has proven itself in the marketplace is an important factor.

3. *Management.* You can have a good location and a good product or service, but if the management is not done correctly, the business will most probably not do well. Conversely, how many times have you seen a business—particularly a restaurant—go out of business, and six months later another food service business moves right in to that same location and "kicks the doors down" with business. Same location, same type of business, better management.

So let's return to my sports analogy of big business (football rules), small business (baseball rules), and real estate (basketball rules). All three are ball games, but the rules of each are very different, and we have to make sure that we're using the right rules for the right ball game. In the next chapter we'll look at what rules are important to you.

8

How Much Can I Make?

WHAT DOES A BUYER really want to know about a business? What does he really need out of the business? He or she needs an income! If I take this job—if I buy this business, if I buy this job—how much will I make? That is ultimately what a buyer wants to know.

The best answer to that is to determine how much the present owner is making, minus the new debt service paid to the seller or to the bank (if you were able to get a bank loan). The new debt service payment of the business has to come out of the existing cash flow. Plus whatever improvements *you* make to your cash flow after the sale.

So, how much does a business make?

Before we apply the rule of thumb, we have to define "small business" for our purposes, which means dividing small business into two sections: those with annual gross sales of $1 million per year *or less*, and those that do $1 million per year *or more*. From now on let's forget big publicly traded business; we do not deal with them. Also, let's call a business doing $1 million or less in annual gross sales a *small business* and those that do $1 million or more a *big business* (both privately held).

Normally, a business has sales growth of 3 to 15 percent a year. The earnings available to the managing owner of a small business is approximately 10 to 20 percent of the business's gross sales. For instance, if a business has $300,000 per year in gross sales, there is potentially $30,000 to $60,000 available to the owner. Gross sales of $400,000 per year would provide from $40,000 to $80,000. I call that the "true owner net," the owner's discretionary cash flow or the recast earnings, or "normalized" earnings plus "perks." I believe the seller who tells me he is making 10 to 20 percent of his gross sales, provided, of course, that he will finance part of the business purchase price based on his warranty and representation. If he won't finance part of the purchase price, I won't buy the business.

Once a business gets above $1 million in gross sales, the earnings potential, or the true owner net, gets squeezed down to 10 percent of gross sales or less very quickly. Any business doing over $1 million in gross sales whose owner is making anywhere near 10 percent is doing well.

True Owner Net

I call the total lifestyle a business provides to the owner and his or her family "true owner net." This is also what is available to a new owner for both new debt services and to live on.

Take a gift shop, for instance, which has a "keystone markup," meaning you buy a wholesale product for $5 and sell it for $10. You double the cost. Let's say the shop does $100,000 in gross sales:

$100,000 gross sales = 100% of sales
− *$50,000 cost of goods sold < − 50% cost >*
= $50,000 gross profit (50% of sales)

— *30 to 40% (business expenses,*
  nondiscretionary expenses, such as employee salary,
  rent, electric bill, phone bill, insurance, etc.)
= 10 to 20% left, available as the true owner net
  (depending on how the owner manages the business)

Now factor in the effects and influence of tax management and expense out depreciation (there is no actual physical depreciation in a gift shop; it's a cash flow shelter); expense out your car, perhaps your spouse's car, auto insurance, health insurance, life insurance; expense out trips to the gift trade market in Atlanta, New York, London, San Francisco, etc.; and perhaps even expense out a family member who gets a small salary or "allowance" for helping out at the store; and this business will probably show a loss for tax purposes. However, the "true owner net"—what's left to the owner after paying all nondiscretionary expenses, the real owner benefit for owning the business—is between 10 and 20 percent of the business's gross sales.

Movies and Pizza

Some businesses will outstrip the 20 percent rule for a while, and then market forces usually take over and reassert the rule. For instance, the best cash flow business I've ever seen in 20 years of selling businesses was the video rental business when it first came out. It blew the top off the 20 percent rule.

The price of VCRs dropped from $1,200 to $200 over a short period of time, and everyone owned a VCR and rented movies like crazy. Remember the $49.95 lifetime membership cards? What a deal for the store owner! They put your name and address in a computer and gave you a membership card that cost 10 cents. Is that a great markup or what—$49.95 for a 10-cent card. Then they would sell you (rent you) a movie that you brought back, which was then sold to the next member for the same rental factor with no additional cost of goods sold. And if you didn't bring the movie back on time, you automatically "rented" it until you did return it.

The video store owners were taking money to the bank in wheelbarrows. Then the market began to get saturated with a video store on every corner, and Blockbuster Video came out and changed the dynamics of the entire industry. Blockbuster opened "megastores"—5,000-plus square feet, 10,000 titles—with neon signs in the window advertising free memberships with a video rental. They had used the favorite word in the English language—*free*—and with their ability to have large, beautiful, well-stocked, and well-run stores open 24 hours a day, 7 days a week, coupled with national advertising, a strong brand name, and stock market money, they quickly dominated the video rental market.

Now, between cable TV, satellite dish TV, home computers, DVDs, movies on demand, and people like my wife Elaine, who buys rather than rents movies after they come back down into the $9.95 range, movies don't get rented nearly as frequently as before. As smart as Mr. Sumner Redstone is, and I am sure he is a smart man, no one can stop a market trend change. Now Blockbuster is in trouble. Great locations, high rent, and, compared to a few years ago, low sales. If it were not a publicly traded company with revenue of stock sales in addition to product or service sales, it would probably have gone out of business. And when you figure the true owner net on a video store, you'll see it's back in the 10 to 20 percent range.

And remember when "they" said the movie theaters would soon go out of business? Well, now theaters are springing up like mushrooms after rain. Going out to the movies is an event, a "date night," and folks enjoy the change and getting out of the house.

But as for those movie theaters, what in the world were they thinking? The same guy who did the market study for the motel business must have done the market study for the theater business. "Let's build another 16-plex, 24-plex, 30-plex rocking chair theater in this suburb." These theaters are huge, they are very comfortable, and they cost $1 million per screen to build. When you go to the movies, there are 28 people in the theater. You can't make that up, even with a $15 bag of popcorn. Almost every major theater chain in America is in bankruptcy. Many are closing. The old rules still apply. You have to take in more in sales than it costs to operate your business or you will go out of business.

You also have to constantly adjust to the market changes and competition. Take the pizza business, for instance. When Pizza Hut first started with "eat-in" pizza parlors, they *owned* the pizza business. Remember the unique roof designs and glass corners? Then Dominos came out and proved that the pizza business was a "delivery" business, and Pizza Hut almost went broke trying to stick to their business model. Now Dominos *owned* the pizza business. Today, all of Pizza Hut's new stores are "take out and delivery."

Then the owner of Dominos made a bad business decision: he decided to become a sports mogul, bought the Detroit Tigers, and lost his focus on the pizza business. He almost went broke. Then he did a very smart thing. He sold the Detroit Tigers to the Little Caesars people. Now they have to run a sports team as well as the pizza business. The good news for Little Caesars is that they know more about the sports team industry—they also own the Detroit Red Wings.

These facts are exactly why I believe that a small business that has been in business three years or longer is a successful business. It has made the necessary course corrections to survive, and the owner must be paying all of his business's bills and making enough in addition to be paying his house payment, car payment, and feeding all his children three times a day. Where else is the money coming from? Out of the "true owner net" of the business, the real cash flow. Now, remember, you can go for years without a profit, but you cannot go a week without cash flow. (And it's probably better not to buy a sports team.)

9

The Cash in Cash Flow

OW LET'S TALK about the *cash* in cash flow! Many small businesses—those with under $1 million in annual gross sales—operate on what I call "checkbook accounting." Revenues are deposited into the company's bank account or checkbook, and expenses are paid out of the company's checkbook. There is one cash register, and the owner receives all income and pays all expenses. What accounting is done uses real "cash," rather than the "accrual" method of accounting that larger businesses normally use. The owner's management style of always being there and controlling the money allows for the reasonable control of the business using one set of books based on the most important book: the checkbook. And percentage wise, they pay far more taxes than many big businesses.

Sales and Other Taxes

On the twentieth of every month, a business has to file a sales tax return with the state tax commissioner, and almost every state has a sales tax (normally from 6 to 8.25 percent of gross sales). That percentage is the amount of taxes due and payable on the twentieth, with the filing of the sales tax report. If Mom and Pop didn't have to file tax returns, they probably wouldn't do that much accounting.

Though the following has never happened in Charleston, South Carolina, I have heard of it happening in other parts of the country. Mom-and-pop small business owners realize that if they don't report quite as much sales, they won't have to write quite as big a check to the state tax commissioner on the twentieth of the month. For instance, if they report $100,000 in gross sales this past month, they have to include a check for $8,250, assuming the higher tax rate of 8.25 percent. Now, if they only report $90,000 in gross sales, they don't have to write quite as large a check.

Having personally sold many businesses over the years, here is what I believe with all my heart: whatever the business owner reported in gross sales and *paid sales tax on*—I believe he did *at least* that amount in sales, and that is the number I can hang my hat on to arrive at the 10 to 20 percent true owner net earning potential. If the owner represents to me and to the buyer that the cash flow or true owner net is between 10 and 20 percent of his reported gross sales, I'll believe that. Once again, provided that the seller will finance part of the purchase price based on the seller's warranty and representation.

What, you say? How could they do that? How could they not keep complete and accurate books and perhaps not report all of their sales? Very well, thank you, is how—and they pay more than their fair share of taxes in other ways. Unlike big business that hires lobbyists to write the tax laws that allow them to expense out all kinds of lifestyle perks, Mom and Pop will have to survive in other ways. And if they are nothing else, small business owners are survivors. They have survived through start-up, they have survived the competition, survived theft from employees and customers, market changes, and the tax man.

They do pay taxes, however, and lots of them. They pay taxes on their real estate property, on their autos, on the furniture, fixtures and equipment, on their inventory; they pay withholding taxes on their employees, unemployment taxes, they collect and pay sales tax on their reported sales, and they also pay sales taxes on everything they buy. They pay taxes on their salary. So you can see they pay more than their fair share of taxes.

Now let's look at an example of cash management in a private business.

Cash Management

Say you and your wife own and manage a dry cleaning business. You open at 7 a.m. and you are in the store until 7 p.m. Today's receipts are $400, consisting of $100 cash and $300 in checks and credit cards. (The actual ratio is almost exactly reversed: $300 in cash and $100 in checks and credit cards, but for our example let's use the $100 cash when you close up. What a day!)

Your wife says, "Let's pick up the kids and go out to eat. I'm too tired to cook." And you don't know how to cook. So you and the family head out to Applebee's or TGI Friday's, and supper costs $46. On the way home you fill your car with gas or fill up your wife's car with gas, and at home one of the kids says he needs $20 for school tomorrow and another kid needs $15. Tomorrow, in the bank line, you have $308 in the bank bag, so you figure you had better keep the $8 for lunch, and you deposit $300 in checks and credit card receipts.

Now, fast-forward to the twentieth of the month, and you are filling out your sales tax report for the month. What do you think the "reported" sales for that day are going to be for tax purposes—$300 or $400? Remember, you have to send that check for 8.25 percent of the reported sales that day.

I'll bet that the reported sales will be $300 for that day.

Now, let's go to Saturday, the busiest day of the week, with folks picking up their dry cleaning for the weekend. Let's say Saturday's sales reached $600 ($200 in cash and $400 in checks and credit cards). You put the $600 in the bank bag and head home. What a week!

You go grocery shopping over the weekend, take the kids to the park, and come Monday morning in the bank line, you have $400 in checks and credit cards for your deposit. Again, fast-forward to the twentieth of the month. What do you think the reported sales are going to be for Saturday? My guess is $400.

Now, I am not saying that it's right or wrong, but this is often how the real world of small business works. Mom and Pop do not run that business to keep accurate books and pay taxes. They run that business to provide a living for themselves and their family.

This example allows for two days out of a six-day workweek. Multiply that by 52 weeks in a year and expand the example for every day of the week. That could amount to somewhere between $15,000 to $30,000 that never went into the business's bank account or checkbook and therefore never went into the business's set of books.

In a bigger business, one with over $1 million in annual gross sales, there is usually no cash that isn't being reported in the books. The big business has the same management style and accounting needs that General Motors does. You cannot keep up with the big business using checkbook accounting. You must operate with complete books, and you must close out everything on a regular basis. This is especially true with multiple locations in a business. Mom and Pop could not possibly keep up with a million-dollar-plus business in their heads by just using checkbook accounting. They would lose control of the business and where they are, and if you lose control of where you are, your employees find out very quickly. You may have some "partners" that you hadn't planned on, or didn't know you had.

Over $1 million in annual gross sales forces a business to have more complete books, and therefore you can recast the financials just like you do with the big business (football) rules. It's all in there. Since the financials are still done to pay no taxes or to minimize taxes, to allow for the owner's lifestyle, I still need to sit down with the owner and get him or her to show me where the "dogs are buried" in the financials. What money is discretionary cash flow? How much can be added back to the "real" bottom line, and therefore what is the true owner net?

The books of a small business, under $1 million, are kind of like the advertisement for Prego spaghetti sauce: "If it ain't in there, it ain't in there." You cannot recast the unreported cash if it never went into the bank and it never went into the books.

So, let's say that the owner of the dry cleaners is reporting $428,000 in gross sales (adding up the 12 months of reported gross sales), and he tells me that he is making $68,000 a year. I absolutely believe that. Based on my 10 to 20 percent rules, you can make from $40,000 to $80,000 per year out of a business doing over $400,000 in gross sales. But if approximately $30,000 of the $68,000 was cash, I'll never be able to *prove* the total cash flow based on the business's books.

When he agrees to finance the purchase based on his warranty and representations, I'll believe him. If he refuses to finance part of the deal, I will not buy it.

More on Small Business and Taxes

As I stated earlier, small business pays more than its fair share in taxes and provides most of the jobs in America. Almost 100 years ago Oliver Wendell Holmes wrote, "Taxes are what we pay for a civilized society." Yes, but today all tax laws are written by special interest groups. Every year, thousands of individuals and companies have incomes exceeding $200,000 per year, and they legally pay no taxes. In the real estate industry, we "wrote the book" on tax deductions—we sell tax shelters.

In 1934, Judge Learned Hand wrote, "Anyone may so arrange his affairs that his taxes shall be as low as possible; he is not bound to choose the pattern which will best pay the Treasury. There is not a patriotic duty to increase one's taxes."

And I always liked Steve Forbes's presidential campaign proposal of a "flat tax." Congress will never pass a flat tax. Do you know why? Because there is a powerful and respected lobbying group dead set against a flat tax. And they are not your ordinary tax evaders. They represent what are called "charitable deductions."

A large portion of the budget for churches, universities, colleges, hospitals, the Red Cross, the Salvation Army, and every other nonprofit organization in the world is based on charitable giving for which they can offer charitable tax deductions as incentive to donate money. And since they do not have to pay taxes, their true owner net is always "before taxes." Now you and I always thought that rich folks who gave big money to the university and to charities were just nicer than we were. We never thought about the tax strategy.

And Steve Forbes has steadfastly refused to give out his personal tax returns. He said it would distort his message. I bet it would! I bet he doesn't pay any taxes, or relatively few taxes, considering his worth. You see, rich folks have tax deductions and tax shelters that we have never heard of. That's why I don't get so upset when mom-and-pop small business owners do everything they can to "legally" lower their personal taxes. After all, they probably pay more taxes on profits than General Motors does.

In fact, let's look at big business as a comparison.

In the last few years some of the "big boys" have ponied up quite a lot of "hush money." Merrill Lynch wrote a check for $100 million. Now, they did not do anything wrong, you understand—it says so in the agreement; however, they paid $100 million so that they would stop asking them questions.

Citibank paid several hundred million, Bank of America about $100 million, and the mutual fund boys paid over $200 million. Now please understand: none of them admitted doing anything wrong. They just decided to pay a few bucks so folks would stop asking them questions. And you were starting to feel a little uneasy about small business?

Now Citibank did an intelligent thing. They hired Sallie Krawcheck, a Charleston girl, to head up their investment banking division, Smith Barney. She is smart, honest, has a stellar reputation for integrity, and she's pretty. Wall Street could use a lot more Sallie Krawchecks.

When I first mention to new brokers in training or when educating a new buyer about the "real cash flow" of a business and how it may vary from what is shown on the business tax returns, they sometimes question the honesty of a small businessperson. Let's put this situation in the proper perspective by using an analogy.

If I had a family farm, and on that farm I raised some corn, wheat, peaches, cows, hogs, and chickens, you wouldn't even question the fact that the eggs my family and I had for breakfast this morning came right out from under the chickens. I did not pay retail for the eggs, and they never showed up in my family's farm books. Neither did the corn, wheat, and peaches my family ate. I run this farm to provide for my family, not to keep books or pay more taxes than necessary. If I started off this year with 10 cows and they had 4 calves and I ended up with 10 cows because my family and I ate 4 of them, you wouldn't think anything was wrong with that, would you? They were my cows!

And if one of my daughters sold some peaches from a small roadside stand and made $350 over the summer for a school trip to Washington that didn't get into the family's farm books, what would be wrong with that? If we decided to trade some produce for products or services, what would be wrong with that? And we also raised our own vegetables and feed for our livestock.

Now, when we harvested the corn crop and sold it to ADM or the Co-op and got a check for $37,825, and got a check for the wheat crop for $49,715, and the peaches brought in a check of $18,023, we deposited all of that in the bank. The farm's books were based on that deposited revenue minus any and all expenses, depreciation, and any and all legal deductions that constitute my family farm's financials. And sure enough, we lost money again, for the eleventh straight year. The personal consumption never went into the books; however, it certainly helped to provide a lifestyle for my family and me. Which is exactly what a family farm is supposed to do.

Since most folks do not have a family farm, the family business *is* the family farm. And they run their business to provide for themselves and their family, just like our grandfathers and grandmothers did when they raised, fed, and educated a family of five out of the corner grocery store that they lived over. You better believe that store never showed a profit for tax purposes; however, it did exactly what a family business is supposed to do: it provided for the owner and his or her family.

Today's family farm is a dry cleaners or a grocery store, a retail business, a restaurant, lounge, convenience store, or auto repair shop, and it's run just like the family farm. If junior comes home from school and needs a new pair of Nike shoes for basketball practice, Dad takes the money right out of the cash register. Sis's piano lessons are paid for in cash or traded out of the business, and the owner's car, his wife's car, gas, auto insurance, health insurance, life insurance are all paid for through the business with *before* tax dollars, not *after* tax dollars.

The business convention often doubles as a family vacation trip, and the family business provides the total family lifestyle for the family; again, just like a family farm used to.

The 10 to 20 percent true owner net formula of cash flow allows for the "cash" in cash flow. It doesn't matter to me if an owner takes out his money in a paycheck, cash, or family perks, the total amount available to the owner of a business for cash flow could be between 10 and 20 percent of gross sales. I wouldn't believe anybody who tells you he is making more than 20 percent on his gross sales, unless he is selling cocaine or something on the side.

For instance, in the food service industry there is a ratio of 28 to 32 percent on food costs, 28 to 32 percent on labor costs, 5 to 10 percent for rent, and another 10 percent for some additional costs such as advertising, electric bill, telephone bill, insurance. This leaves an owner a true owner net of from 10 to 20 percent of gross sales, depending on management.

The best thing to do is to let the owner "recast" the financials and explain how he manages the business for his family in order to represent the true owner net or cash flow and the total advantages of owning the business.

So to restate an important point: if an owner (seller) of a small business represents to me or to you that he or she is making between 10 and 20 percent of gross sales (and for a larger business, 10 percent of gross sales), I'll believe that—provided (once more) that they will finance the purchase of the business based on the warranty and representation. And if he or she won't finance part of the purchase price, beware!

10
Buyers

MOST BUYERS OF BUSINESSES in America today are not entrepreneurs in the true sense of the word. Entrepreneurs are "risk takers." *Risk?* I don't want to take any risks! This is my life savings for goodness sake. This investment *has* to work! I've found that most buyers are what I call "forced entrepreneurs." They probably have a better chance of making a good living for themselves and their families by going into business for themselves than they do by just getting another job, especially if they are over 40 years old. There are not a lot of $70,000 to $80,000 per year jobs out there in today's economy. To make that kind of money, or an equivalent lifestyle, you probably need to own your own business.

A motivated buyer is probably not one who has a job but says, "I always wanted to own my own business." It's more likely that a truly motivated buyer doesn't have a job and is burning through his $60,000 in life savings. Every month he delays finding another job or starting or buying a business, he has about $4,000 less in savings. The next month he has $56,000, the month after that, $52,000, then $48,000. That's a motivated buyer, and he probably fits the profile. And, all things considered, his best option is to buy a business.

The 90 Percent Rules of Buyers

If you are a golfer, 90 percent of the time you do better when you stay within the fairways, don't you? What follows is a list of what I like to call 90 Percent Rules of Buyers, some of which were written by Tom West and some of which I have added over the years. I try to do all of my training and educating on what I call the 90 Percent Rules. Most of the time they will serve you well.

1. 90 percent of buyers are first-time buyers. In other words, they have not been in business for *themselves* before. They are not risk takers, and they are not just investors.
2. 90 percent of buyers will have to *finance* the purchase price of a business, just like we had to finance the purchase of a house, a car, a boat, or most other big-ticket items.
3. 90 percent of buyers are *not sure* what type of business to buy or what best serves their needs.
4. 90 percent of buyers are *scared to death* because owning their own business is new to them. For the first time in their adult lives, they don't have a job, and if the husband is afraid, the wife is petrified. ("How are we going to make the house payment, the car payments, feed and educate the children?")
5. 90 percent of buyers will have to get the *sellers to finance* part of the purchase price. So if you look at Rule 2, above, which says 90 percent of buyers will

finance the business, the logical question is: where's the financing coming from? Answer: the seller, whether they want to be the source of financing or not.

6. 90 percent of buyers will *not buy* the business that they called about—they are just starting the process of elimination. And most decisions, big and small, are a constant process of elimination.

7. 90 percent of buyers have from $15,000 to $60,000 in the "Hip National Bank" that they are *willing to risk* or to spend by investing in a business. They may have a net worth of considerably more, such as owning a house valued at $300,000 with only a $100,000 mortgage; owning stocks or bonds that they do not want to sell in the present market, or they have $100,000 plus in a 401(k) retirement account. All of which add to their net worth, but none of which a buyer will normally wish to risk to buy a business.

8. 90 percent of buyers are used to and are very comfortable making what I call a *10 percent decision.* They'll pay 10 percent down on a house or car, and as long as they can make the payments affordable, they don't care what the price is. However, buying a business is going to take most of their life savings and most of their time and attention. Therefore, it is not a 10 percent decision; it is much closer to a 100 percent decision. It's kind of like getting married. It's a 100 percent decision, which is one reason why it is so scary.

9. 90 percent of buyers are from *35 to 55 years old,* have come out of middle management with a company, and are used to making from $45,000 to $95,000 per year.

The good news is that I believe you can sustain a lifestyle comparable to an income from a job of $45,000 to $95,000, less tax, out of most of the existing businesses and franchises in America today. Provided that they have been in existence three years or longer and have a successful track record with annual sales growth from 3 to 15 percent or more.

You know why I am comfortable saying that? The present owner has a house payment, car payments, children to feed and educate just like you do, and he or she has been paying bills successfully right out of the existing business. How do you think they have been sustaining their lifestyle? In the real world, I believe that you can make a living for yourself and your family out of owning this business for the very reason that the present owner has been making a living for himself and his family out of the business for several years.

All things considered, if you buy this existing business and continue to run it as the present owner has been running it, you should be able to make the same living (income), less the new debt service, of course. The new debt service, whether it is paid to the seller, to the bank, or to the SBA, has to come out of the business's earnings or cash flow. Where else can it come from?

So, when you are negotiating to buy a business, both the buyer and seller must be aware that the new debt service has to come out of the "real" cash flow, or true owner net, and still leave the buyer enough money to live on, or the deal will not work. And neither the buyer nor the seller wants that to happen.

Negotiating the Business Deal

In negotiating a business deal many things are important, but none more so than the price and terms. Part of the price and terms is the all-important *down payment*. This is a "down-payment-driven business," and by and large the down payment is influenced much more by how much money the buyer has and will risk than by how much the seller wants or how valuable the business is.

In the real world, a buyer cannot pay more money down than he or she has or can raise, no matter how much the seller wants. Unless there is bank financing—and most of the time there isn't—the amount of the down payment is driven by the buyer. And remember, if you can buy a business for a $40,000 to 50,000 down payment and make $40,000 to $50,000 per year every year and have the business pay the debt service, that is 100 percent ROI (return on investment) "plus" every year.

And there is nothing magic about the terms and conditions of the balance. The monthly payments have to come out of the cash flow of the business.

So if a seller represents to you that he is making $50,000 per year out of the business and that number fits into my 10 to 20 percent rule (in other words, the business is doing at least $250,000 to $500,000 in reported gross sales), then you can believe him, provided he would finance the purchase. However, you cannot agree to pay the seller $3,000-per-month payments just because that's what he wants.

You cannot take $3,000-per-month debt service payments out of a business that makes $50,000 per year, unless of course you can live off $14,000 per year (which you can't). You are setting up a deal that will not work for either party, buyer or seller. The monthly payments have to be payable out of the cash flow, leaving the buyer enough money to live on, or it won't work. Unless, of course, the buyer can grow the business or better manage it to get additional true owner net.

Also, the down payment should never take a buyer out of cash. He must have some working capital to carry the business for a while, even though an existing business should have an immediate cash flow. You also have to make house payments, car payments, and so on. Although the seller always wants more down payment and the buyer would always prefer a smaller down payment, somewhere in between the two there is a fair deal, a level playing field, that will work for both parties, or we won't have a sale.

Finding a Good Business for Sale

Since you cannot put out a sign on the business that says, "For Sale," as you do with real estate, and since there is no multiple listing service for business sales because of confidentiality, how do you find a good business for sale? Often when you look in the "Business Opportunities" section of the newspaper or under "For Sale by Owner" you will be "bottom fishing." Most good businesses are not listed under "For Sale by Owner."

My suggestion is to contact a business broker—just as you would normally get a good real estate broker to help you find the right house and a good stockbroker to help you buy the right stocks. The business broker has hundreds of businesses for sale in all types of industries: retail, service, manufacturing, distribution, food service, dry cleaners, coin laundries, liquor stores, and franchises. And since buyers normally pay no fees, the services of a business broker are free to a buyer.

Obviously, I recommend calling a Sunbelt Broker in your town because I trained them; plus, they have continued professional education as members of our industry trade association, the International Business Brokers Association (IBBA), and many of them have obtained the industry certification of Certified Business Intermediary (CBI).

If you cannot locate a local Sunbelt Business Broker, I recommend calling another member of the IBBA, since all members subscribe to the organization's Code of Ethics. I am confident that, while business brokers almost always work for the seller, they will treat all parties fairly and honestly and assist buyers in finding the right business. Because if a buyer doesn't buy a business, the seller can't sell a business, and remember that a deal *must work* for both the buyer and seller, or it won't work.

Usually, you will find business brokers listed in the yellow pages of your phone book under "Business Broker," and you will find specific businesses for sale in your Sunday paper under "Business Opportunities" or "Businesses for Sale." If a broker runs the ad on the business, the ad must state that and identify the broker or the brokerage firm handling the sale.

Another way of finding a business for sale is on the Internet. The Sunbelt Web site is www.sunbeltnetwork.com, and you will find a list of our offices and over 10,000 businesses and franchises listed there. This is the closest thing business brokers have to a multiple listing service to market the businesses they have for sale. However, because of confidentiality, you probably will never be able to look at an ad in the newspaper or on the Web that completely and specifically identifies the business.

Add to that the 90 Percent Rules that buyers do not know what kind of business they want or will best serve their needs, and 90 percent of the time they are not going to buy the business they first call to inquire about, and 90 percent of the time they do not know anything about baseball (small business) rules—and you come back to the same advice. Call a business broker and find one with whom you feel comfortable, who takes the time to meet with you, gets to know you, encourages you to get to know him or her, and educates you about the real world of small business.

Again, in that recommendation, I'm suggesting the same thing as if I were recommending that you buy a house or stocks. In those cases I'd say find a broker with whom you are comfortable and ask their assistance in finding the right house or investment. Even though real estate brokers normally work for the seller, they know the market, they know about financing, and they can help walk you through the maze much better than you could wander through it on your own.

Also, don't be a "day trader." Work with a broker. Certainly, express your preferences and help direct the broker to your wishes, but also take advantage of the professional broker's experience and knowledge. And he or she has hundreds of businesses to choose from.

The Importance of Relationships, Again

The meeting with the broker and the meetings later with the seller must be *face-to-face*. Buying a business is too important and personal to be done over a fax machine or by phone or e-mail. Those technologies may have some application, may save some time and facilitate the sales process. However, relationships take time to build and must be personal.

Occasionally when I am talking with a buyer he'll say, "Just fax or e-mail me the information on the business," or, "Just fax or e-mail me a Confidentiality Agreement and I'll fax or e-mail it back." I won't do it; it just won't work that way.

I cannot help you find the best business for you without meeting you in person and trying to accomplish four very important things:

1. *I need to get to know you*, your background, your preferences, your lifestyle, your financial needs, and your comfort level of financial risk.
2. *You need to get to know me*, my experiences, my background, my understanding of the industry, the marketplace, businesses for sale, available financing resources, and the latest trends in business.
3. *I need to take the time to educate you* about the real world of small business. Almost nothing in your background can prepare you for small business (baseball rules). There are no absolute rules of value, there is no bank financing, the financials never look good, you've got to make an offer to get started and negotiate, etc.
4. *I need to get you to sign a Confidentiality Agreement* requesting you to keep all of the information that I give to you about a specific business confidential and to keep confidential the fact that the business is even up for sale. Also, I will keep your information confidential.

Now, all four of these things are very important; however, if you had to pick the least important, which one would that be? You may have guessed it, but if not, the answer is the final item, the Confidentiality Agreement.

The other three things can be accomplished only with a face-to-face meeting. It is just like looking at a business: you have *got* to go see it, and if you have any interest at all, you have to meet with the seller face-to-face to let him or her tell you about the business; how they got started in it, what's presently going on, about the future of the business, and why they are selling.

So much of this decision is going to be based on your "gut feelings" about the broker, the business, and the seller, and the only way to have enough information is through personal meetings, exchanging a lot of information, and asking a lot of questions.

I would not deal with a broker or a seller who would not meet with me and take the time to help me in all aspects of this major decision. If you cannot arrive at a comfort level with the broker, the business, and the seller, then I would not recommend buying the business.

Remember that you are the buyer, you are the customer, and ultimately the buyer drives the deal. If the deal doesn't work for you and you don't buy it, then the seller has not sold it. So the first thing to accomplish is to find a broker you are comfortable with, then find a business you are comfortable with—one that you feel you can manage with the proper training and transition from the seller or the franchisor. Then get an accountant and a lawyer whom you also feel comfortable with and follow the next steps covered in the chapters that follow.

If you do not go through a broker, you still must have a comfort level with the seller and, of course, the business, and I'll show you how to protect yourself throughout the process. However, I always recommend a business broker because he or she understands the process, has a good knowledge of the local market, and can help you navigate the many obstacles and work out a deal structure that works for you and for the seller.

11

Focus Is Crucial

Look at the Business, Not the Financials

Throughout the business buying process, I ask my buyers to keep their *focus on the business, not on the financials*. The financials have been done with one purpose in mind: to pay no taxes or to minimize taxes. They have not been prepared to show how well the business is doing or to even be a fair portrayal of the value of the business. In fact, they have been done for just the opposite reason: to show that the business is not doing well for IRS purposes. I cannot change that fact, and I cannot change the financials. They are set in concrete. What I can change, hopefully, is the buyer's understanding of what he or she is looking at when studying the financials.

"Well, can't you recast the financials like they do in big business," you say, "and rebuild the seller's discretionary cash flow, the EBIT or EBITDA?"

Yes, but you cannot recast the "cash" or the "owner's perks" that never went into the financials in the first place. You cannot add back what is not in the financials. Remember the Prego spaghetti sauce reference: "If it ain't in there, it ain't in there."

So focus first on the business—location, FF&E (furniture fixtures, and equipment), inventory, employees, industry, competition. Is this a business that you would like and feel confident you could run?

What's the Top Line?

The second area of focus is when we finally do see the financials: *focus on the top line, not the bottom line.* The only thing the bottom line on business financials reveals is that the seller has a good accountant or doesn't. The top line (gross sales) tells me a great deal about the business. It tells me the market's response to the business's product and/or service. It tells me the trends of sales and if there is a large enough top line—based on my 10 to 20 percent rule—to give me enough of a bottom line to live on and to pay back my debt service.

Another real-world example about the usefulness of the top line is this: At Sunbelt, I've done many appraisals for the courts. I have been certified as an expert witness on business valuation in dozens of court cases. When there is a divorce situation, for instance, and the husband and wife are fighting over the value of a business, the judge or the attorneys often need an expert opinion. Usually the husband goes into court with the financials and the tax returns, holds up the returns and says, "Your Honor, this business is not worth anything. Here are my tax returns for last year; we lost $16,000."

The judge is a lawyer, of course, and lawyers don't know anything about the value of a business, so he thinks, "Wow, they lost $16,000. I don't see how this poor devil is still in business."

Then, of course, the wife gets a chance to speak, and she says, "Your Honor, I do not know anything about the financials, but I'll tell you this: Judge, this is a very valuable business. It has been the only source of income for our family for the last 15 years, and we've always lived in a nice house, driven nice cars, taken a vacation every year, sent our children to college, and even had enough left over for this bum to run around with his _____!'"

"Order, order in the court!" yells the Judge.

You know what? They are both telling the truth. It is a very valuable business; it has provided a good living for the family for years, and it lost $16,000 for tax purposes this past year. When you are looking for value, look at the top line, not the bottom line.

The 10 to 20 percent rule is also a very real constraint. You can make $50,000 out of a business that is doing $250,000 to $500,000 per year in gross sales; you cannot make $50,000 out of a business that is doing $100,000 in gross sales.

And at the appropriate time we will see the "recast" financials to let the seller re-present the "real bottom line" or seller's discretionary cash flow or true owner net, not just the bottom line on the tax return.

The 70-30 Percent Ratio

The third area of focus is what I call the "70-30 percent ratio." Most of the weight of the buyer's decision (70 percent) should be based on what the buyer feels he or she could make based on how they would run or manage the business *after* they buy it. The smaller weight of the decision (30 percent) should be based on how the seller *has run* the business over the past few years.

For instance, if you are looking at an existing dry cleaning business, what can you do about how the seller has run the business for the last several years? Not one thing. Look at what you can change to make the business better. How would you run the business if you owned it? That is what you need to focus on.

Consider the following example.

Let's say you're having a buyer/seller meeting and you ask the seller, "Mr. Seller, I noticed that you don't have a drive-through drop off at your dry cleaners. Do you think it would be a good idea to put in a drive-through?"

The seller will probably reply something to the effect of: "I've thought about a drive-through, however the building configuration doesn't lend itself well to a drive-through, and besides, my customers know that I don't have a drive-through so I don't believe it would make any difference."

Oh yeah? There are a lot of people, women in particular, traveling with small children or animals in the car, who are just not going to do business at a dry cleaners that doesn't have a drive-through, especially in bad weather.

Another question might be, "Mr. Seller, I notice that you close at 6 p.m. Do you think it would be a good idea to stay open a little later?"

The seller says, "I get here by 6:30 a.m. and by 6 p.m. I'm tired and I want to go home, and besides, my customers know that I have always closed at 6:00, so I don't think that it makes any difference."

Oh yeah? In a lot of families, both the husband and the wife work outside the home, and with the rush hour traffic in the city, they don't even get home until after 6 p.m., and therefore they don't stop at your dry cleaners because they can only pick up their clothes on Saturday.

Sam Walton figured that out years ago. He said, "You know what? It seems a lot of families have both the husband and wife working all day so they don't have time to do the shopping between 9:00 and 5:00. We need to keep all of the Wal-Mart stores open late enough to let folks get home from work, feed the children, and then go out shopping. We need to keep all of our stores open until 9 p.m., then 10 p.m., then 12 a.m., and some stores are open 24 hours."

Mr. Sam did something pretty radical. He decided to run his business based on *what his customers wanted*, not what he wanted. Because of that fact, he sucked up all of the business. The mom-and-pop stores that said, "We have always closed between 5 and 6 p.m.; our customers know that, it plainly says that on the door"—many of them are now permanently closed. More on Mr. Sam in Chapter 12.

One other question for the seller might be, "Mr. Seller, have you ever sent out any coupons in your market area?"

He'll probably say, "No," or, "Yes, we did that once in 1998; it seemed to work, but it's a little bit of a pain to keep up with." Or he might say, "You probably ought to do that. If I were just starting out, I would probably do it."

Another question for the seller is, "Do you attend the industry trade shows?" Probably not.

Guess what? The buyer buys the business after some serious negotiations, with owner financing. He takes over new management, and he is full of enthusiasm.

He puts in a drive-through by laying those little drive-over "ding-a-ling" bumpers that allow him to come out to a customer's car if they want and to pick up orders, give receipts, deliver orders, and pick up payments at curbside. He stays open one more hour, until 7 p.m., to allow folks to pick up clothes or drop off clothes on their way home. And he sends out coupons to every household within a five-mile radius of his store by zip codes. He adds wedding dress preservation to his service, alterations, and valet service to surrounding hotels and motels. He learned how to do all of this efficiently at the industry trade shows.

The coupons announce that XYZ Dry Cleaners now has a "drive-thru" and that they are open until 7:00 every night for your convenience, Monday "thru" Saturday, and that they have a special on shirts for the next 60 days.

Guess what, again? What do you think is going to happen to the sales of the business? Yep. They are going up with a very small increase in costs. The new buyer is paying the same amount of rent, same employee costs (he and/or his family are the only employees staying there to work the extra hour), the same FF&E (furniture, fixtures, and equipment), but he is growing his top line while his fixed costs remain constant, which gives him more of a bottom line.

So most of the weight of the decision to buy the business (70 percent) should be focused on what the buyer is going to do with the business *after* the sale. The new buyer often brings fresh enthusiasm to add to the old owner's experience, and there is nothing better than enthusiasm. Even the word *enthusiasm* is good—it's derived from the Greek word meaning "with God."

You pay the seller for what he is doing with the business now, not based on the potential. However, you buy the business because of the potential.

A Simple Business Plan

The following one-page plan for a small business focuses on the top line and what you would do to improve the business. (I like one-page plans, one-page agreements, one-page contracts, and one-page letters.) I suggest you use it on any business you are looking at, and certainly you can expand it as needed.

Business Plan for [Name of Business]

I.   List five things about the business that you would continue to do:

      1.

      2.

      3.

      4.

      5.

II.   List five things that you would change or eliminate to improve the business:

      1.

      2.

      3.

      4.

      5.

III.   Variable True Owner Net (dependent on your management):

      Gross Sales $\times$ 20% = _____ (High range)

      Gross Sales $\times$ 10% = _____ (Low range)

      Total of Low and High Range

      _____ $\div$ 2 = Average   _____

      Plus employee salaries you

         and/or your family would

         be picking up   + _____

      Less any note payments back to

         seller or bank for financing   − _____

      Your True Owner Net   _____

IV.   Why would this be a good business for me?

      _____

      _____

      _____

Think about that one-page analysis. As I keep pointing out, the single most important decision that you make in life is whom you are going to marry. You don't sign a 58-page contract drawn up by the smartest lawyer for the most important contract in your life. (Though it might take a 58-page agreement to "get out" of a marriage.) Where are you going to live? Will you have children? How many children? What are you going to do? What is your spouse going to do? Who knows! You simply "show up," walk down the aisle in front of a broker (preacher or justice of the peace), and say, "I do."

My point is that simplest agreements are often the best because it's people who have to make a contract work after the deal, no matter what is in the agreement. It's what is in your heart and head that counts, not the words on paper. You have to work hard to make the deal work!

In every partnership contract I write I add the phrase that "all parties to this contract will use their best efforts and talents, both learned and God-given, to make this a successful venture for all parties involved." While it is not legally binding, it goes to the spirit of the agreement, which is most important. As we go forward in this relationship, just as in marriage, we cannot possibly "spell out" all the possible circumstances that may occur. Let's just agree to do our very best to work together to make things work for everyone.

Now let's look at some small business that worked *big-time.*

12

Success Stories

S O MANY BIG BUSINESSES started out as small businesses and, through a series of management "course corrections," one business would do very well and another business in the same industry would not do as well. Let's look at some of those business stories, which I call "War Stories."

Every business has a story, just as every person has a story. And there is a lot more to a business story than just the financials. The financials are only one small chapter.

For instance, an important chapter in the story of a business might be the location. Another chapter might be the FF&E (furniture, fixtures, and equipment) that produced the product or service; another might be the inventory that the business sells. Still another important chapter would be the one about employees. (How many times have you heard the expression, "The main assets of the business walk out the door every day at 5 p.m."?) And then there's the chapter about the industry itself and the future of the business in the industry. The trend of sales would be a chapter, as would a discussion of the competition. Price and terms of a business's sale would be a major chapter, and oh yes, one very important chapter would address the financials of the business—but that would be only one chapter, as I have already pointed out. I used to call the financials chapter "Chapter 7," but that's a bankruptcy chapter, so let's call it "Chapter 6." It sounds a whole lot better.

One of the problems in seeking the advice and counsel of an accountant or in attempting to get a bank loan is that the accountant and the banker often only look at Chapter 6 to make decisions—only one chapter in the business story book—and miss the "rest of the story," as Paul Harvey says. Do you not agree with me that all the above-mentioned chapters are important "value drivers" of the business—not just the financials?

Here are a few business success stories that have a lot more to do with the management/owners than they do with just the financials.

Story 1: Sam Walton and Wal-Mart

I had the pleasure of visiting Mr. Sam's original store, Walton's 5&10 in downtown Bentonville, Arkansas, about 3:30 a.m. one morning when I was nearby doing the opening training for the Sunbelt office in Fayetteville. (My friends Carl and Kathy Grimes own the office there, and they are a perfect example of why there is so much success through good people and good relationships, business and personal, in northwest Arkansas.) It was about a 16-hour drive from Charleston.

I called my wife Elaine when I got in (as I always do) and told her I had just seen Sam Walton's original store and had finally arrived in Fayetteville. It was 4:30 a.m. in Charleston, and she didn't seem nearly as excited about my seeing Mr. Sam's store and the Wal-Mart home office as I was. She politely suggested that I call her later and tell her all about it. She had given me a copy of Mr. Sam's book, *Made in America*. Some of what follows is paraphrased from Mr. Sam, and some was garnered from watching Wal-Mart grow.

Mr. Sam said that he had never had an original thought and that he constantly sought ideas from other retailers and "stole or borrowed" the best ideas and best practices he found. He was a constant observer of business when it came to making "course corrections." Sam did not invent retailing; he did not invent discounting. When he first started, Sears or Kmart could have squashed him like a bug.

Mr. Sam started out as a licensee or franchisee of Ben Franklin Stores, and when he couldn't get a store where he wanted to live (northwest Arkansas), he decided to go into business for himself. He liked Bentonville because of the local folks and the other small towns that he could expand to. He also liked the fact that there are three states that meet in that area (Arkansas, Oklahoma, and Missouri), and that it was a good place to raise a family and (with a staggered bird hunting season) a good place to hunt.

One of the main problems he and other retailers had—particularly "discount" retailers—was "pilferage," "shrinkage," or whatever else you want to call employee and/or customer theft. Back then, they did not have electronic monitors, like they do today at every exit door.

When you did catch someone stealing, instead of just solving a problem, you began a new problem. You made an entire family of customers mad. When you catch a customer stealing, his or her dad comes down to the store, furious, ranting and raving, saying something like, "My son wouldn't steal anything from your stupid store," and of course you have to say, "I know he wouldn't, but he had a lot of stuff accidentally stuffed under his jacket when he was leaving." Fortunately and unfortunately you caught a shoplifter, but you lost him, his parents, aunts, uncles, and cousins as customers.

Out of the several stores that Mr. Sam operated, one in particular had considerably less shrinkage. He flew down in his plane to pay that store's manager a visit and see what this manager was doing right or differently from what other managers were doing. You want to know what the secret weapon was? A greeter. He had a "greeter" at the door of his store.

Now shrinkage is probably not why the store manager had hired the friendly retiree to greet shoppers at the door. A lot of times in business, as in life, you make a minor change that results in a major course correction. The original greeter was a retired veteran, and he probably talked the manager into giving him a minimum wage position to help around the store with whatever odd jobs needed to be done to allow him to get out of the house. Everyone at Wal-Mart was paid minimum wage at that time.

However, being friendly by nature, and probably knowing most of the folks in the town who shopped, when his chores were all finished, the vet headed to the front door and greeted customers as they walked in. "Good morning." "Good afternoon." "How are you all doing today?" "Thanks for shopping with us."

Mr. Sam considered the greeter to be the single best business idea he ever got. When you look someone in the eye and pleasantly welcome them into the store and thank them for shopping, two things magically happen. First, they think, "The person who greeted me saw me come in here and could recognize me. I'd better not steal anything from this store." Second, the customers realize that these people are nice, and that if they are going to steal something, maybe they'll go down the street and steal from the other store that doesn't take the time to say hello and be nice to its customers.

Either way, it worked! Mr. Sam put a greeter in every store immediately, either a retired man or lady, and shrinkage went down as front door customer relations went up. Less shrinkage went directly to Wal-Mart's bottom line and gave them a real advantage over the competition.

Then followed another small, but ultimately powerful, human relations course correction at Wal-Mart. Mr. Sam noticed that the minimum wage employees were not outgoing or very effervescent; they were somewhat introverted and reserved. Even so, they were careful to follow company policies. So Wal-Mart set up this company policy: if a customer comes within 10 feet of an employee, the employee should greet them, ask them if they need any assistance, and thank them for shopping Wal-Mart.

Wow! Look at the difference between a Wal-Mart and a Kmart in that one seemingly small but important area. If you ask someone in Kmart where something is, you usually are interrupting, because they're busy doing something else. You have to hunt an employee down and say, "Excuse me, excuse me, but can you tell me where X is?" Probably they can't, but if they do happen to know, they'll say, "I think it's on aisle 14," and then they zoom back to whatever important mission they were working on before you came along.

When you ask someone in Wal-Mart where something is, you know what they'll do? They will take you to the item personally and then thank you for shopping.

One of the above-mentioned companies has constantly been on the brink of bankruptcy and recently did file for bankruptcy protection, under Chapter 11. The other is the largest retailer in the world. They are both discounters, they are both known-name "megastores," they both sell Igloo coolers and Coca-Cola and Pepsi, they both have state of the art point of checkout inventory systems, distribution systems, and great buying power. The difference is in the management.

Another major difference between Wal-Mart and Kmart is that Mr. Sam stocks his stores in the daytime, while customers are there. This means more employees to interact with customers, and "activity begets activity." Kmart stocks their stores at night, after hours. When you go in to shop in the morning at Kmart, the store is neatly well stocked, but there are no people around to say "Good morning."

One other difference among giant retailers that I find fascinating has to do with Sears. Before Wal-Mart really started growing, the largest retailer in the United States was Sears, and Sears has steadfastly refused to have one small item present in their stores: *shopping carts*. Think about it. When you shop at Sears, once you have an item in one hand and another item in the other hand and you can't carry anything else, you are done shopping. You are heading to the checkout and out to the car. If you are shopping with a small child or several small children, once you have your only free hand filled, you are done shopping. Wal-Mart, Kmart, Home Depot, and the local grocery store all have shopping carts so you can shop freely and don't have to be limited in your purchases by what you can carry. You can even put a toddler in the shopping cart, which makes for a more pleasant shopping experience.

Now why all the MBA geniuses in the Sears Tower in Chicago can't figure that one out, I'll never know, except that they still do not allow shopping carts. I guess they are counting on people with multiple sets of arms, bigger shopping bags, and stronger biceps. Maybe they need to put a housewife on their board of directors.

And one other major difference in the success of Wal-Mart over its competition goes to the very heart of this book. Wal-Mart is a family business. Wal-Mart has an "owner family" that we can relate to. We shop at Mr. Sam's store, and we feel like we know his family. His wife and children, his brother Bud, and the rest of his family are all a major part of the Wal-Mart success story.

Who owns Kmart anyway? Who owns Sears? Faceless stockholders. We don't know who the ever-changing management team is either. They aren't business owners, they are hired management folks. We feel that we know the people who own Dell Computer, Microsoft, Charles Schwab, AOL, CNN, McDonald's, Kentucky Fried Chicken, Wendy's, Ben & Jerry's, and we know their stories. We can relate to them as regular folks just like us, who owned a family business and made it big. Good for them, and good for us! Americans love winners and success stories. We in turn support them with our business and our loyalty.

Story 2: Colonel Harland Sanders and Kentucky Fried Chicken

While I was driving up Interstate 75 to do the opening training for Brian and Stephanie Mazar, who are the Sunbelt office owners in Louisville and Lexington, Kentucky, I noticed a sign reading "Corbin, Kentucky, 2 miles." Recognizing Corbin as the birthplace of Kentucky Fried Chicken, I decided to visit the Colonel's original store.

Do you know why Colonel Sanders started Kentucky Fried Chicken? The highway department built an interstate, I-75, and it missed his motel and restaurant on U.S. Highway 25 in Corbin by about two miles. It put him out of business.

Did he stop? No, he made a course correction. He auctioned off his motel and restaurant and barely got enough money to pay off his debts and mortgages. Then he and his wife took his first Social Security check proceeds and went "on the road" selling recipes for a special way of cooking chicken that everyone in the world would like. The rest, as they say, is history.

One life and business touches a lot of others, doesn't it? Colonel Sanders was no exception to that rule, although he certainly was an exception. One of the folks he touched is another great businessman and a wonderful person. (Or at least seemed to be, as I didn't get the pleasure of meeting him in person before he passed away. See next story.)

Story 3: Dave Thomas and Wendy's

Dave Thomas was an orphaned child. He says he never knew who his birth parents were, but he was raised by the most wonderful folks in the world. He has done a lot for other orphans; he believed, as I do, that we are all God's children.

Dave did not finish high school. He dropped out in the tenth grade. As a teenager, he worked in a restaurant and enjoyed the food service industry. Back then, most restaurants were the full-menu type: steak, pork chops, chicken, roast beef, fish, hamburger, etc. However, he noticed that most of the customers seemed to like the fried chicken that was cooked with Colonel Sanders' recipe.

Dave and a few other folks came up with the rather radical idea that you could have a successful restaurant that served only fried chicken, mashed potatoes and gravy, green beans, baked beans, macaroni and cheese, coleslaw, corn on the cob, and biscuits.

Awww, come on, Dave. Now, sure you can have a fast food program built around hamburgers; Ray Kroc had already proved that with McDonald's, along with Burger King and Hardee's and some others, but just fried chicken? That will never work!

Mr. Dave and a few others proved that you *could* have a fried chicken restaurant, and he was one of the original Kentucky Fried Chicken franchisees with multiple, successful operations.

Then he came up with another radical idea. He felt that even the very competitive fast food hamburger market could use another franchise that focused on better quality (never frozen) hamburger meat and real chicken breast sandwiches (not just chicken "parts"—remember the great ads, "Parts is parts" and "Where's the beef?"). Many folks said Wendy's, named after his daughter, would never work.

After 35 years, Dave Thomas decided to go back and finish high school. He did, and his class voted him "Most Likely to Succeed." Good choice; he owned about 4,000 restaurants at the time.

Story 4: Arthur Blank, Bernie Marcus, and Home Depot

You know why Arthur Blank and Bernie Marcus started Home Depot? They got fired from their "regular jobs." They had to make a course correction. When Bernie called up a friend and told him that he and Arthur had been fired and what had happened, his friend said, "Congratulations, Bernie, you just got kicked in the ass with a golden horseshoe. Now go out there and start your own business." And that is exactly what they did. You may have heard of their business.

Incidentally, Arthur and Bernie wrote a book about the beginnings of their business, which they sell at Home Depot. Not surprisingly, it's orange and it's called *30 Billion Dollars in 20 Years*. Now is that growing a company or what? The book costs only $19.95! Americans will buy anything for $19.95. Everything you see for sale on TV costs $19.95, or three easy payments of $19.95. ("What is it? I don't know, but it's only $19.95 so let's get one!")

They opened up what we call a "big box store." Home Depots look as if they have $10 million in inventory in the store the day they open up. I guarantee that the 80 percent/20 percent rule applies to Home Depot, just like it does anywhere else. Eighty percent of their sales come out of 20 percent of their inventory. Then why don't they just carry the 20 percent of inventory that they know sells?

Well, because Home Depot's main draw is what they call a "big box." They've got just about anything. If you want a $3 hammer or a $300 nail gun, or some nails, come to Home Depot. They've got it. If you want to hang some wallpaper or fix a door, the "tradespeople" the Home Depot hires as employees can show you how. Home Depot helped develop this market.

When Home Depot first started, only about 8 percent of people did "do it yourself" projects around the house. If a light switch didn't work, you called an electrician. If your sink was leaking, you called the plumber; for a leaky roof, the roofer. After 20 years of helping folks and holding seminars on "how to do it yourself," Home Depot has turned America on to the idea.

One other thing about business folks learning from other business folks. You know where they got one of their best basic ideas about marketing? Mr. Sam Walton.

When Home Depot first started growing, they would depend on special sale items to get customers through the door. However, there was a huge problem managing inventory correctly for special sales. If they featured a sale on leaf blowers in a store in Virginia, for instance, how many units did they need—200, 300, 700? Sometimes they would run out, and sometimes they would create large amounts of overstock after the featured sale.

Mr. Sam advised them to get away from the special item sales, as Sears does, and instead develop an acceptable competitive markup that gives great value for everything and makes them the low-cost provider on all items in the store all of the time. That way, the customer doesn't have to decide whether to go to this store or that store today to take advantage of a special sale. They simply say, "We need to go to Home Depot or to Wal-Mart to get some things we need." And after they get you there, the management knows that you just might find some other items that you cannot possibly live without. (Put them in the shopping cart.)

Ever notice the main messages in Wal-Mart and Home Depot ads? They are value, low prices, *and* smiling, helpful employees. That was no accident—it was a course correction. Speaking of course corrections, I always liked the NASA story about the first man on the moon. Did you know that the first moon landing successfully landed within 15 feet of the designated landing spot? Fifteen feet! Wow! However, the rest of the story is that they made approximately 86,000 course corrections from takeoff to landing. Business, life, and space exploration require a constant set of course corrections.

13
Sellers

Why Sell?

At Sunbelt, as at most business brokerage firms, we have existing businesses for sale in all areas. Retail, service, manufacturing, distribution, food service, lounges, coin-op, liquor stores, and others, in all sizes and locations. We also sell hundreds of franchise opportunities, new and resale. In addition, we sell main street businesses ($1 million in annual gross sales or less) and larger businesses ($1 million to $30 million in annual gross sales). One thing all of our listings have in common is that they have a seller, and they have a business story or history and a track record.

An existing business usually has the advantage of a track record at that location. It has survived three years or longer and has an established customer base, cash flow, and trained employees. It has furnishings and equipment that produce and distribute a product and/or service and has established vendor relationships. The business also has a record of producing enough sales to pay the business expenses and provide for the owner's personal expenses and lifestyle.

However, if this is such a great business, *then why is it for sale*? Why would an owner be selling a perfectly good business that is serving its purpose, providing a living for the owner and his family? What is wrong? A buyer always asks that question of a seller, and so do I as a broker.

In most cases, what's wrong is a result of a personal situation or circumstance. For instance, the owner is retiring; the owner or a family member is unfortunately in poor health; the seller or owner dies, is getting a divorce, or relocating; the owner has decided to pursue something and cannot do the business 8 to10 hours per day as well. Sometimes the reason for selling is as simple as the owner being "burned out" and wanting to do something different for a living. If he has only been open six months and he tells you he's burned out—look out! However, real burnout after 5, 7, to 15 years is a very real reason for selling; it's like the seven-year itch.

It's the same phenomenon as when homeowners move from one perfectly good house to another: there was nothing at all wrong with the first house, they just decided to move to another one. Sometimes we change jobs, locations, wives, husbands; things just *change* as we go through life. Sometimes the change results in a need to sell a perfectly functioning business that has been providing for the owners, just as it is supposed to.

That is life. But I always want to honestly know why the owner is selling. And the buyer also wants to know, and has a right to this information. If I wasn't completely comfortable with the seller's story about why he or she is selling, I would be very cautious about proceeding with a purchase. That's another reason why I want the seller to put his money where his mouth is and finance part of the purchase price.

What about the seller's "exit strategy"? Exit strategy! What exit strategy? Small business owners don't have an exit strategy, or if they do, it's a plan to go down the highway, turn right onto the interstate, and head south. Most business owners are too busy running the day-to-day operations of the business to plan an exit strategy. Then one of the human-driven changes comes up, and the business—particularly the financials—have not been prepared for an exit. That may be good, not bad, since you want the business to continue on its successful course with a seamless transition of ownership. The business continues; the seller quietly exits.

Buying and Selling Franchises

A franchise has the advantage of a recognizable brand name and a proven system of operations that has worked well in other locations. The market has responded well to the franchise's product or service, and the other franchise owners are successful and pleased with their investment in the franchise. A franchise is a partnership of sorts, a shared investment that establishes an ongoing relationship between franchisor and franchisee. Both parties have privileges, responsibilities, and obligations to each other. Franchising has proved to be a very successful method of growth for many, many businesses in all sorts of industries. It works, and it's a method of being in business *for yourself,* but *not by yourself.*

Here's an example most of you will recognize. Whether viewed as a historical or religious figure, Jesus in many ways can be seen as the most successful franchisor in history. He grew his "business" by recruiting and training his franchisees (11 out of 12 of which were successful—what a great track record), and they started to spread His teaching and messages regionally at first, then nationally, then worldwide. His systems and trainings have changed the world. In fact, the very calendar that most of the world lives by is a result of Jesus's life (BC/AD).

From a business standpoint, a franchise is a known name and a system of business operation that teaches you how to produce and sell your product and/or service throughout your market territory. It is a proven system of business success that is teachable and trainable, can be duplicated and repeated, and that the marketplace responds to by purchasing your product or service. The individual franchisees are local owner/managers—a tactic to ensure that the system is followed faithfully, allowing the success in one area to be duplicated and repeated in other areas.

Also, a franchise may be attractive to a buyer who came out of middle management of a big company. He or she might have been vice president of X. They went to work every day, and they managed successfully inside this X box. The training people took care of training, the P.R. people took care of P.R., the R&D people took care of R&D, and the finance people took care of finance.

When you buy a franchise, they train you initially and then you go to work every day and manage inside this box just as you did in your last middle-management job. When you come from that background, it's likely that buying a franchise fits your comfort zone. As before, the training people take care of training, the P.R. people take care of P.R., the R&D people take care of R&D, and the finance people take care of finance.

Also, unlike an existing individual business, the financials are complete because the franchisor's systems are tied into the cash register, gross sales and the top line, not the bottom line, so the corporate office can assist you in managing correctly and monitor your success. Often, they share in your success through royalty payments, so you both have a vested interest in your success and prosperity. You both have a vested interest in staying on the leading edge of the market trends in your industry.

One of many good things that result from a franchise business relationship is that, unlike private individual business where the accountant and lawyer will not recommend that you buy the business because of Chapter 6 (the financials are not complete or accurate), the lawyer or accountant may very well recommend that you buy a franchise for several reasons. First, they have heard of the franchise, and they perceive it to be successful. Second, the financials balance, and "it's all in there." Third, the UFOC (Uniform Franchise Offering Circular) is required by law for every franchise operation and gives the professional the basic information necessary to recommend that their client purchase that franchise.

Guess who buys a lot of franchises? Accountants and lawyers. Banks, also, may make a loan or finance the purchase of a franchise for some of the same reasons listed above. Up to 95 percent of franchises are still in business after five years. A franchise's success rates provide a very strong underpinning of value, which also corresponds with a lower risk.

A franchise resale has the advantage of the franchise's known name, system of operations, specific track record at that location, trained employees, existing customer base and cash flow. The financials should be accurate and complete, and you should develop a comfortable relationship with the selling franchisee or business owner and the home office or franchisor. Both relationships are very important to your success.

Again, that brings up the question of why the seller is selling. It's a question whose answer we always want to feel comfortable about. I would also want to talk with some other existing franchisees of that franchise as part of my due diligence and ask these further questions: "If you had to do it over again, would you buy this franchise? Are you happy with the franchise and are you making a living?" Even if I got all of the right answers, I would still require some seller financing in a franchise resale, just as I would in any other small business acquisition.

Sunbelt has partnered with one of our brightest, successful, young franchisees, Scott Evert, in Minneapolis, to develop a specific program to assist Sunbelt offices with franchise resales. We have developed a program to build relationships with major franchisors to let us assist them when one of their franchisees wishes to sell. We are the only company that has an office in every city.

So if you want to sell an Ace Hardware store in Omaha, Nebraska; in Sacramento, California; in Fort Worth, Texas; or in Nashville, Tennessee, we have an office there to assist you. Former Speaker of the U.S. House of Representatives Tip O'Neil used to say, "All politics is local." Well, I say, "All small business is local too."

Also, look in the mirror before you buy a franchise. Can you follow a system and do it their way? Or are you too much of an independent "cowboy" and only want to do your own thing? In the latter case, franchising may not be the best match for you. That is not to say that franchising is right or wrong, just that asking yourself that question will show you the best way to go with your own business decision.

Here's a good test. Were you an A student in school, a B student, or a C student? If you were an A or B student in school, you would be a good candidate for owning a franchise. The A student usually excels at following directions and doing what is expected. The B student can also be a good franchise owner candidate. But C students usually are not good candidates, because they don't like to follow directions.

The A student usually does an excellent job in top management of a company or in running a division of a company for B students, who are often the president and do an excellent job of managing for the C students, who probably *own* the company!

The C students are cowboys, and they do better when breaking all of the rules, not following them. (Get these cows from Fort Worth to Kansas City—how to get them there is up to the cowboy.) They are also survivors. Dave Thomas dropped out of school altogether (although he returned as an adult after succeeding in business), Thomas Edison never graduated, Henry Ford was not a good student, Bill Gates and Michael Dell dropped out of college, and Ted Turner? I bet he was a C student.

About two years ago Sunbelt began focusing on new franchise sales for other franchise companies, and we represent and introduce their franchise opportunities to the 250,000-plus buyers we see each year. This adds quality inventory to our marketplace. In 2004, Sunbelt sold more franchises than all the other business brokers put together.

Mergers & Acquisitions: Selling Big Businesses

In the world of small business, a business doing over $1 million in annual gross sales is a big business, and one doing $20 million to $30 million is a *huge* business. Many business brokers do not handle $5 million to $30 million companies. This is what we call Mergers & Acquisitions, or M&A, deals, which might bring to mind the investment bankers, stockbrokers, and high-powered deal makers you see on TV. Even at the industry trade group, the IBBA, most folks handle "main street business brokerage." There is a group of experienced and professional brokers who are IBBA members and also members of the M&A Source, and they focus almost entirely on the middle market of $5 million to $30 million and more.

While it has not been the primary focus of Sunbelt over the first few years of our franchise life, things have changed. Since many Sunbelt franchisees are very successful in "middle market" M&A deals, in addition to "main street" brokerage, we have opened Sunbelt Private Investment Banking, LLC, as an M&A division. And many of our Sunbelt brokers are members of M&A Source.

Bigger deals require financing. No buyer can write a check for several million dollars out of "Hip National." Often, banks are much more comfortable with a business doing $3 million to $30 million in annual gross sales. And in the larger transactions, many buyers invest some cash and some stock in acquiring the company. This is a whole different set of rules than with small business—this falls under football rules.

One of the best things to happen to me and to Sunbelt (in addition to the wonderful and bright brokers who have joined Sunbelt as franchisees) is that we are becoming players on the M&A field. It happened that as Sunbelt became the largest business brokerage franchise in the world, with over 200 locations (currently we have reached over 300 offices), about half the calls my partner Dennis and I were getting from our franchisees had to do with M&A deals. Our office owners were being contacted by owners of businesses that were doing $5 million to $30 million in gross annual sales, and they were looking for a broker to assist them in the sale.

The brokers would call me and say, "Ed, I have an appointment with a gentleman tomorrow who has a business that is doing $22 million in sales. What do I do?"

Of course I would say, "Go list it, we might sell it."

Although this is an apt example, I know that selling a multimillion-dollar company is a different business from main street brokerage. Therefore, I attended the annual IBBA meeting in Atlanta, Georgia, in 2000 to learn more about M&A so I could add that to my broker-training curriculum.

As fate would have it, there was a misprint on the schedule and a meeting that was supposed to be held on Thursday, taught by one of the top M&A instructors in the IBBA, Ken Hoganson from Chicago, was not being offered on that day, but earlier in the week—and I'd missed it. However, Sunbelt is always an exhibitor at the IBBA conferences, and Ken came by our booth. We have a little AAA road map in our exhibit that has red pins to show our locations around the country. Ken took a look and said, "Wow, you guys have certainly grown." I said, "Yep, the Lord has certainly blessed us, and we have a location in almost every city."

I then told him how sorry I was that I'd missed his course. I explained that I needed to train my brokers in handling bigger deals, but without losing our focus on the main street businesses. I told him that we wanted to be the "Home Depot of business brokerage." If the buyer wants a $3 hammer or a $300 nail gun, it will be one stop—Sunbelt's got it! You want a small business, large business, franchise or franchise resale, one stop, call Sunbelt Business Brokers; we have the inventory, experience, professionalism, and honesty to treat you fairly and help you find a business. I was on my soapbox.

We started talking, and being the wonderful teacher that he is, Ken said that he'd be glad to help us learn the M&A process and to assist us in any way he could. I'm pretty good at pushing the envelope, and I always try to partner with folks who I feel are smarter than me and I can learn from.

I asked Ken how many M&A deals he handled in a year. He said "Eight to ten, on average."

"How would you like to do *a hundred*?" I asked. "If you join with us and help teach our Sunbelt M&A division how to do our part to manage the sale and close the deal, we'll have something to offer that no one else has—the expertise of one of the nation's top M&A specialists and 1,500-plus M&A broker agents in every city, all over America."

Well, the upshot of that conversation is the new entity, Sunbelt Private Investment Banking, LLC (M&A Division). Someone else can send out a letter; at Sunbelt we send out a professional broker. We have the close relationship of a local brokerage office and the best M&A team in the business. From the Engagement Package, to the Confidential Memorandum, to the M&A appraisal, to the marketing book, to the growth plan, to the universal search for prospective buyers, to managing the showing, negotiations, letter of intent, due diligence, final bid and closing, we have it all. Many of our offices now focus on M&A.

We can work with the seller's team and the buyer's team of professional accountants, lawyers, bankers, etc., to get the deal done in a way that is positive to both buyer and seller. Add that to main street brokerage, franchise sales, franchise resales, business financing, seller-financed note guarantees, consulting and development, and Sunbelt now offers a full menu of business services.

14

Valuation Methodology

AMERICANS LIKE to have an answer to the question, "What's the value?" What's the value of a business, car, home, investment, etc.? Usually, we equate price with value when it comes to most of our purchases. At the checkout counter of the grocery store or at Wal-Mart, Kmart, or Office Depot, the clerk runs the tag through the scanner and we pay the total price. For 95 percent of the things we purchase, the price is the value. As I stated earlier when discussing negotiations, we, as Americans, usually either pay the asking price or we don't purchase the items.

In buying a house, we arrive at a value by looking at comparable prices of houses in that subdivision or market area based on square footage, features, location, amenities, condition, and so on. However, we can come pretty close to arriving at market value based on comparable and competing properties—and remember that the banks are going to underwrite at least 90 percent of appraised comparable value. So, I can pretty well tell you what the value of the house is. One of the main things that upholds that value is the fact that you can buy a house with only 10 percent down. Who cares what the house costs? What's the down payment, and what's the monthly payment? If we can get you financed, then we have a deal.

What is the value of a car for sale? The "blue book" will give you a market value of every type of automobile based on model, year, mileage, condition, etc., from both the retail and wholesale perspective. So, I can pretty well tell you what the value of a car is. And often the bank or finance company will finance a major part of the purchase. And nobody cares what the car costs, they care about the down payment and the amount of the monthly payments.

To prove this, let's look at how they sell cars. "Low down payment, no down payment, $1,000 cash back, no payments until next year." The monthly payment has to be under $500 per month on a car and under $1,200 per month on a house. To keep payments under $500 on a car, they went from three-year financing to four years, to five years, to seven years. When that didn't work because the price of the car kept going up, they came up with more ingenious plans. "We won't sell you the car, we'll rent the car to you (lease sounds better)— you don't own it, of course, but who cares?—the payments are always under $500, and you have a low down payment." Now if the price of cars keeps going up, buyers will have to put a Porta Potti in the back and finance it for 30 years while they live out of the backseat.

When the Federal Reserve raises the interest rate and the price of real estate keeps going up, the only way to get the monthly payments back down is to extend the terms (40 years, 50 years, etc.). And why not—no one lives in a house for 30 years anyway.

Valuing a Business

What is the value of a business? It depends. I can do a good job of arriving at a business's value based on several appraisal methodologies: multiple of earnings, multiple of EBIT, multiple of EBITDA, adding up the value of the hard assets plus one- to two-year earnings, discounted cash flow method, comparable business sales, etc. However, no matter what method I use, there's no guarantee that *that* business will sell or that it will sell for that price.

You see, there is no third party or bank financing to uphold 75 to 90 percent of the market value or appraised value or comparable value that I have determined. So first I have to find someone who wants that business (that dry cleaner, retail store, restaurant, auto repair shop) in that section of town. Then the market will determine if the business will sell, what it will sell for, and at what price and terms. The buyer, the seller, and the market drive the decision about the value of the business, and the market drives the price and terms of the deal.

In that one area a big business—a publicly traded business—and a small business—mom-and-pop—are exactly alike. What is the value of a publicly traded company? It is not based on the value of its inventory, the value of its FF&E, or a multiple of the EBITDA. The value of a publicly traded company is what the market (stock market) says it is, and that value is subject to wide and significant change. Although you bought shares of that company for $86 per share several months ago, that may have absolutely nothing to do with the share price and value of the shares (therefore the value of the company) today. It may be worth more; or it may be worth less, as a lot of folks have found out over the past few years. Either way, it has a market-driven value that may or may not have a direct relationship to valuation methodology.

A small business is just like that. I can do a very good appraisal of value based on the industry and the specific business. However, that does not mean this specific business will sell, and it does not mean that it will sell for that price. One of the best approaches to value is to get an arm's length, certified, third-party appraisal on the business before we take it to market. The appraisal serves as a "sanity check" for market value, as my friend Dan Elliot, the Sunbelt owner in Houston, Texas, calls it. The appraisal will also be necessary for any bank and/or SBA financing. However, it is ultimately the market that will determine value.

The market value is what a ready, willing, and able seller (under no duress to sell) will sell for, and what a ready, willing, and able buyer (under no duress to buy) will pay for a business. Since both have knowledge of the market and value, the terms and conditions of the sale have to be agreed to by both buyer and seller. A good business appraisal normally will be very close to market value.

When you add in the fact that I'm normally not dealing with a foolish buyer (nor do I want to be) and that I'm not usually working with a foolish seller (nor do I want to be), the market value works pretty well. The terms and conditions have to work for and be agreeable to both parties. However, in some cases, either the seller or the buyer may be under some pressure (duress) to sell or buy, and that could affect market value.

The buyer cannot put down more of a down payment than he has in "Hip National Bank," or than he can get; and the debt service on the balance, whether to the seller or to the bank, must be paid out of the business's cash flow. In addition the buyer must leave him- or herself enough to live on after all the business's bills are paid.

The seller has to agree to the terms and conditions also, or the business will not sell. Which means of course that if he does not sell, he still has to get up at 5:30 every morning and go open the dry cleaners, and the buyer is still burning through around $4,000 a month of his life's savings since he still does not have a job or source of income. A no sale is not good for anyone.

When we do arrive at a price and terms agreeable to both parties, that is the market value. And incidentally, a good business broker will add significant value to the deal for both the seller and buyer to help get to market value.

From the seller's standpoint, a broker can expose the business opportunity to hundreds of prospective buyers without employees, customers, or competitors knowing that the business is for sale. The seller can go right on running the business and keeping everything profitable and attractive while the broker does the work of searching for a buyer and managing the myriad things that have to be taken care of in a business presentation and sale.

From the buyer's standpoint, how would you even find a good business that is for sale? There are no signs in the window saying "Business for Sale" or a multiple listing for businesses for sale that specifically identifies a business. Also, how would a buyer learn about "baseball rules" and understand how to look at the real value of a business, or figure out how to finance a business, or how to make an offer and negotiate, without the assistance of a broker?

When your accountant advises you not to buy a business, your lawyer advises you not to buy the business and your bank banker won't lend you the money—that's great except for one little fact: you still don't have a job and you still don't have an income. Those professionals have not helped you solve your problems. And next month you have $4,000 less in savings at Hip National Bank.

The business broker will help you find a solution to your problem, and it's a good solution. They will help you find a business and help you negotiate and buy it based on terms and conditions that work for you. If you wish to buy the business and do buy it, you may have a job for life. You have the opportunity to grow the business and to possibly make more money than you would at a job, and you should have something of value to sell when you wish to sell.

The good and well-intentioned folks at the SBA, including the Small Business Development Center, and SCORE (Service Corps of Retired Executives) actually know very little about small business. As I stated earlier, these well-intentioned and sincere academics and retired big business executives do a great job with business plans and start-ups, but they seldom know anything about the real world of baseball rules (small business). They will look at the books of a dry cleaner who has been in business for 12 years and say, "I don't see how this is going to work. Look at the financials."

What do they mean it won't work? It has obviously been working for 12 years or his doors would be shut. The owner has been paying his payroll every Friday, his rent every month, and his vendors on time or they would have cut him off. He's also made his house payment, car payment, and fed and educated his children, or he would not still be there. The SBA folks, accountants, and lawyers are all missing the forest for the trees. They would rather show you how to "start up" a business, do a business plan, keep good books, and run it as they were taught in college classes and big business seminars.

They also never heard of owner financing and never understood the value of making a seller put "his money where his mouth is," the way you do in baseball rules. These folks are great football players, but this is not a football game.

The value of the business is what the value is to you as an owner or prospective owner. Will this business provide a living that works for you; can you pay off the business debt in three to five years out of cash flow? If so, how much is it worth?

Below, we'll discuss some of the Rules of Thumb or Field Formulas that I've used successfully to arrive at a "ballpark" value of a business. Then the terms and conditions of a specific business sale still have to be worked out between the specific buyer and the specific seller.

Recasting the Financials

All of the formulas are based on some "multiple of earnings" or "true owner net" for the existing business, and based on the most recent year's sales. Sales drive value, *sales drive value!* If there are no sales or low sales, then the business has no value. If there is no top line, there can be no bottom line. Don't forget the 10 to 20 percent rule. It works very well for small business (under $1 million in annual gross sales); 10 percent or less for middle-sized businesses (over $1 million in annual gross sales).

All formulas have to be appropriate to sales, however. The sales of a business—product and/or service—are the market's response to that business's product and/or service.

The furniture, fixtures, equipment, and inventory should always be included in the sale at the "normalized" levels because the FF&E and that normal level of inventory are what produced the annual sales. They are part of the sale. When the new buyer closes the deal and goes to open the business the next day, the business should be ready for operations, ready for business as usual.

For the larger businesses (over $1 million in annual gross sales), the financials are normally all-inclusive, and no cash is left out. The buyer would have to sit down with the seller and let him recast or normalize the financials to add back to the bottom line all areas of owner's discretionary cash flow, usually including the owner's salary, any additional family salaries paid to nonproducing family employees, and all owner "perks" such as an owner's car, wife's car, children's car, insurance on the cars, health insurance, life insurance, and trips the family takes. Usually you can also add back in depreciation, the debt and interest costs that will not be a cost to the new owner, and any unusual "one time" cost or expenses that will not reoccur.

This restructuring of the financials to show the real value of a business—its seller's discretionary cash flow—or real total owner's benefit or true owner net or real earnings is called *recasting*.

When the recasting or normalizing is complete, I will have a true owner net that the business is providing the owner, and usually I will value that business at two to five times the true owner net. In other words, if the true owner net were around $300,000, then the business would have a range of value from $600,000 to $1.5 million.

Some businesses may have a specific multiple, but from a "Rule of Thumb" approach, I would be comfortable with a two to five times multiple, following which specific negotiations would determine the final price and terms and whether or not it will sell.

For the main street businesses (under $1 million in annual gross sales) the financials are not usually all inclusive. The owner's cash may not be depicted in the business's books, and therefore cannot be recast or added back to the bottom line. I would use a "top line" approach to true owner net in a small business. The following formulas also lend themselves to the real world of small business in that we'll have an *asking price* based on gross sales that may be considerably different than the *selling price*.

Gross Sales Formulas

In small business, there will usually be severe discrepancies between what the seller wants and what the buyer can and will pay; however, the value is still determined using the gross sales as a basis. Out of the top line comes the bottom line. Here are some specific examples. I call them "Gross Sales Formulas."

- *Retail business (gift shop with Keystone markup).* 70 percent of gross sales would equal the asking price; 70 percent of the asking price would equal the selling price (approximately 49 percent of sales).
- *Food service (restaurants).* 60 percent of gross sales would equal the asking price, 60 percent of the asking price would equal the selling price (approximately 36 percent of sales).
- *Service business (lawn care, janitorial).* 50 percent of gross sales would equal the asking price; 50 percent of the asking price would equal the selling price (approximately 25 percent of sales).
- *Equipment intensive business (coin laundry, dry cleaners, printing company).* 100 percent of gross sales would equal

an asking price (lots of equipment); and it probably will sell for approximately 70 percent of the asking price (70 percent of sales).

- *Manufacturing (Americans like manufacturing companies; they carry the highest multiple).* A manufacturing company or machine shop may very well list for and sell for 100 percent plus its gross sales, especially if it has a "proprietary product" or a "patent" that the market ascribes value to (100 percent or 100 percent plus of sales). However, you also now have to factor in the effects of globalization: Is this a business whose product or whose customer's product can be produced much cheaper overseas?

- *Liquor store (inventory intensive).* There is not much of a markup in the liquor store business, normally only 15 to 22 percent on cost, so a liquor store will usually sell for the inventory, at cost, in the store at the closing, plus around two year's true owner net. The true owner net in a liquor store is not 10 to 20 percent; it is never more than 10 percent of gross sales.

- *Convenience store, with gas.* I do not ascribe any value to gas sales (outside sales); gas is a commodity, and the "big boys" control the price; when you think of it, that is the only business where you put the price "right out" on the street so customers can see it before they pull in. If the store across the street is charging $1.58 per gallon of regular unleaded gas, you cannot charge $1.70 per gallon and compete successfully.

The value of a convenience store comes from "inside sales." The markup on inside sales is normally 28 to 45 percent, and in some cases, such as processed food semi-prepared on site (fried chicken, nachos, hot dogs, popcorn, etc. (no celebrity chef here!), the markup is perhaps even more. Also, there is great markup in fountain drinks and coffee. So if anywhere near 50 percent or more of gross sales in a convenience store come from inside sales, you've got a valuable store.

I'd value a convenience store at the 70/70 percent formula based on inside gross sales; plus the gas inventory in the ground at closing, at cost, plus 5 percent of lottery sales if the store sells lottery tickets (the gross sales of the lottery are not included at all).

Any other business would probably fit the 70/70 percent formula unless there are some unusual circumstances. Sellers always want as much as they can get, of course, and buyers would like to pay as little as they can. Somewhere in the middle is a fair deal that works for everyone; however, the sale price has to be appropriate to the business's sales and earnings. Not the value of the equipment, not the value of the inventory. Once again, if there are no sales, then there is no value.

When you look at the Rule of Thumb formulas, you'll see that they are also a multiple of earnings. If the normal earnings on a small business are 10 to 20 percent of gross sales (average 15 percent), the two to four times earning will put you in the same ballpark of value. However if we do not have complete financials to recast, the sales approach—top line— may be the best approach in small business.

General Motors has to have sales; Home Depot has to have sales; IBM, Lucent Technology, Nortel Network, and Microsoft have to have sales. So why are the stock prices (market value) down on so many of these publicly traded companies, especially technology and computer related companies? Their sales are down, and sales drive value. Lucent

Technology and Nortel have the same FF&E they had, the same inventory of products they had, the same patents, the same employees. What happened? Their sales are down, thus their value is down. (Now they have fewer employees.)

Opportunity Value

Another way to arrive at the real-world value in a small business arena is to look at the *opportunity value*. In buying a business, you are buying an opportunity to make a living for you and your family. The opportunity that you are buying just happens to be a business opportunity.

The best business opportunity may not be the perfect business. A perfect business is already running at 99.5 percent of its potential. You cannot improve the management that is already in place, and there is no upside potential to increase the sales of the business. Also, if the business is perfect, the seller is going to want top dollar to sell.

The best business opportunities may very well be the ones that are chugging along at about 35 to 40 percent of their potential. You can buy it for the right price, add your learned and natural talent to managing the business, and run it up to 99.5 percent.

Here are some examples. I consider a McDonald's to be a perfect business. It's already at 99.5 percent, and I do not believe that you could run a McDonald's restaurant any better than they do already. The store is always located in the best location; it's open from 6 a.m. to midnight; the food is good (may not be good for you, but it tastes good); the store is always clean and well lit; there's sufficient parking; the friendly, well-trained staff usually takes your order correctly and does so quickly. Not to mention a marketing program that other restaurants would kill for. McDonald's partners with Disney, for goodness sake. The kids will beat you over the head to go to McDonald's.

You cannot improve upon the current business operations of a McDonald's; therefore, you cannot make any more money than they are presently making. You cannot sell any more product than is already being sold from 6 a.m. to midnight. A McDonald's restaurant normally does from $1.25 million to $1.5 million in gross sales, yet we are seeing even this success story operation go out of business in many locations for the first time. Here's why: Food costs have gone up, labor costs have gone up, inventory costs have gone up, energy costs have gone up, property taxes have gone up, insurance costs have gone up, marketing costs have gone up—and they still have to sell a Big Mac for what they sold it for 10 years ago. They still have to sell Value Meals for under $5. They cannot raise their prices, and they are maxed out in sales.

Today, the investment in a McDonald's is approximately $1.5 million, and you might make $100,000 per year as an absentee investor. I do not consider that a good investment. However, it will work as a mom-and-pop owner-managed business where the owner gets the $45,000 per year manager's salary and his or her partner gets the $36,000 assistant manager's salary. Add that to the $100,000 net profit and this brings us back to how McDonald's started—the owner/operator franchisee puts in 14 hours per day and makes the business work for them, for their family, and for McDonald's.

Here's another business opportunity: Let's take a hypothetical business that is not being managed to its full potential. The owner is tired, in poor health, playing too much golf, running around with his head waitress, hasn't changed the menu in years, and is being chased by the IRS. In addition, if he has more than one location and cannot manage more than one successfully, he has a problem. Or—another scenario— the owner dies, is getting a divorce, etc. Or this: it is a closed restaurant. *A closed restaurant.* The seller may now owe the landlord $25,000 or more in back rent. There's $200,000 in furniture, fixtures, and equipment sitting inside. The equipment people are due money on their equipment. The present owner is gone, perhaps because of some of the poor management or circumstances mentioned above. The landlord and the equipment people are suing the present owner/tenant for funds due.

Why do you think that they haven't taken the equipment back out of this store? Two (real-world) reasons: (1) What are they going to get for used equipment, and where are they going to store it? Just as well store it in the restaurant. And (2), the landlord says, "Ain't nobody taking anything out of this store until somebody pays me $25,000 in back rent." We have what I call a "Texas showdown." An unresolvable, never-ending dispute.

Now comes a buyer. He has only $25,000 that he can put down on a business. He needs to make a living for himself and his family. So, we put a deal together with a $25,000 down payment. Most of which goes to the landlord, less the broker's commission, of course, and a reasonable note with monthly payments due to the equipment folks. Nobody is quite whole, but everyone wins.

The landlord has part of his back rent and a new tenant who is going to stay and pay. The equipment people have something coming in for the used equipment, and that's better than a kick in the britches. Even the previous owner (seller) comes out for the better: at least the harassment for the rent and the other business debts has stopped. They weren't going to get any money out of him anyway—he's broke. Even the lawyers aren't going to get paid on that deal. And that poor devil has enough problems already, between his ex-wife and the waitress and all.

And guess what? The buyer, for a $25,000 down payment and a small note, just bought himself a business opportunity that, if he works hard and manages correctly, could make him at least $25,000 per year, every year, for the rest of his life. He may even be able to make much more and then have something of value to sell when the time comes. That's a 100 percent return, plus, on his investment *every year* for the duration of his ownership.

Also, if he has a family, they would be able to eat at the restaurant. And if he hires some of his children and they steal food from him—so what? Since he has to feed them anyway, better to feed them at wholesale prices, rather than retail. (Now if any of the other employees take food, that's stealing, and that's not right.)

I maintain that if you can buy a business opportunity, in the form of an existing business or franchise, and you can make back each year whatever amount you invested in down payment, that is a 100 percent return on your investment every year. All things considered, that's a good business deal. The total purchase price is not nearly as important as the down payment. Can you make a living out of the business after the down payment and debt service? That is what I call the ROI (return on investment) on a small business, and that is the opportunity's value. The opportunity to make a living for you and your family.

CPAs come up with different rules for ROI. They deduct a normal manager's salary for that business from my definition of ROI. They say that the manager's salary is not a part of their return. Okay for them, but I say, in the real world of small business, if you are the manager and that money goes into your pocket, then that's part of your return. It's your money and these are baseball rules!

15

Protect Yourself

A Level Playing Field

A BUSINESS DEAL needs to work for both the buyer and the seller or it probably will not work. There needs to be what I call a level playing field or a win-win situation.

Now both buyer and seller are taking a risk, and to some extent they have to take a "leap of faith" in the sale. The buyer is risking his down payment or note or debt service, hoping he can make a living out of the business. The seller is risking that he may not get paid on the balance due to him, unless the buyer is successful in the business and pays him. Hence my theory that in business, $UCCE$$ $OLVE$ ALL PROBLEM$! If the buyer is successful, he will pay the seller and *everyone wins*!

Let's say that we have a business deal where, after negotiations, we end up with a purchase price of $100,000 with $40,000 down payment and a note back to the seller for $60,000 payable over 60 months at 7 percent interest:

Selling price: $100,000
Down payment: −$40,000
Balance: $60,000 note to seller, payable over
                       60 months, at 7% interest

In many cases the buyer will be using a large portion of his or her life savings or family money to cover the down payment on the business. So who is running the largest risk, relatively speaking? The buyer or the seller? *The buyer.*

Should the buyer lose, he loses the down payment and the business assets. If he doesn't pay the seller and the seller forecloses, then the seller gets the down payment and the business back, which he can resell. So even though they are both running a risk, usually the buyer is running the larger risk.

So how do you help ensure a level playing field between the buyer and the seller? Here are several important tips that work for both buyer and seller. Remember that if the buyer can't buy, then the seller can't sell. And I always recommend using former President Reagan's wise adage, "Trust, but verify!"

1. Find a broker who you feel comfortable with even though he may be an agent of the seller. He will not work against you as a buyer. Also, find an accountant and an attorney with whom you feel comfortable. All of them are professionals and will assist you; however, the ultimate decision and responsibility will be yours.

2. Find a business that you like and would feel comfortable managing, providing that the seller or franchisor will teach you, assist you, and train you on how to manage the business successfully.

3. Review the sales, trend of sales, and the owner's story about why he is selling. Study the industry in general. Is it a business that has a product or service that has been and will be accepted by the marketplace? Ask the owner what the business is like and how much he is making. If his response fits the 10 to 20 percent

rule, I'd believe him, as long as he is financing part of the sale. Ask him why he is selling, and see if his reason passes your "gut feeling" test.

4. Make an offer based on terms and conditions that work for YOU, no matter what the seller is asking. The down payment must be what you can comfortably put down, and the debt service must come out of what the seller says he's making and still leave you enough money to live on. You should buy a business based on what the seller is doing now, not based on the future potential of the business. You buy the business because of the potential, but you pay for what the business is doing currently (present day value).

5. The offer should be in writing with a $1,000 no risk, refundable deposit of money to be held by the broker in a trust account, totally and immediately refundable to you should you decide not to buy the business subject to any of the following contingencies.

6. Any offer should have at least these contingencies to protect you and the seller. "This offer is contingent on the following":

   a. Buyer review and approval of the financials of the business

   b. Buyer review and approval of the terms and conditions of the lease

   c. Buyer review and approval of any and all "in place" contracts and/or agreements with employees, vendors, and/or customers

   d. Buyer being able to obtain any necessary financing

   e. Buyer/seller agreement on an acceptable training and transition period for new management

f. Buyer review and approval of any and all franchise documents and approval of the transfer by the franchisor (for a franchise)

g. Buyer/seller agreement on an acceptable industry noncompete agreement

Note: Several of the contingencies are "walk away" clauses as big as a barn door for a buyer; however, that's the only way I'd recommend making an offer, subject to wide open due diligence and the ability to withdraw an offer for any reason if the buyer chooses to at this point of negotiations.

The terms and conditions of the purchase price should be clearly and simply stated. Try to keep the transactions as simple as possible. They can get complicated—all the more reason to begin with simplicity.

For instance, let's say that the seller is asking $250,000 for the business with $125,000 down payment. You may feel that is a fair asking price or a little too high. Most of the time the seller is asking more than the market will bear. (Of course he is, he wants as much as he can get.) I don't blame him. He's selling his livelihood, his "baby."

If you had approximately $50,000 in Hip National Bank that you could put down on the business, I'd suggest that you offer the seller the following: $195,000 total purchase price with $40,000 down payment and the balance of $155,000 paid over 120 months at 7 percent annual interest. I would put the offer in writing with a $1,000 refundable deposit subject to the contingencies above and subject to due diligence. Give the seller three days to a week to respond to the offer.

Is the seller going to be happy with this offer? Absolutely not, and that's a little bit of an understatement. However, it is a serious offer and it's in writing with a deposit, which shows that you are a serious buyer and that you really want his business.

Is it your best offer? I hope not—never make your best offer at first. The seller will almost never take your first offer. I don't blame him; he thinks his business is worth more, and it probably is. However, hopefully he will make a counteroffer (in writing) after some rather unkind remarks about your offer and perhaps some questions about your birth's legitimacy; however, we have "started the dance."

The counteroffer is almost always less than the asking price and may be closer to the selling price and terms that the seller will take. Now if there are other buyers who want the business and will pay more, you may have to adjust your offer considerably. If you are the only and best buyer, the seller has a decision to make. Does he want to keep getting up at 5:30 a.m. and opening the business, or does he really want to sell it? We'll find out.

Now that you have a counteroffer, when you are doing your due diligence you may have a much better idea of the target of value, terms, and conditions that your due diligence will verify. Many times, without an offer to get a deal off center, you do all of your due diligence based on the asking price of $250,000 with $125,000 down payment. That's a "no sale" every time. For one thing, you don't even have $125,000 down payment.

An offer in writing is the first step or first bridge that has to be crossed on this journey of buying a business. If we cannot get across this first bridge, the rest of the bridges don't matter.

Don't be afraid to make an offer that works for you. See what the seller responds with and be prepared to counter the seller's counter. Remember the "absolutes," which are: you cannot pay more down than you have or can get, and the cash flow of the business (what the owner says he's making) must cover the debt service and still provide a living for you and your dependents.

Hopefully, after one or two offers and counteroffers, you are in the ballpark of acceptable terms and conditions. Then you are ready to complete your due diligence. Why spend several weeks or months, hundreds or even thousands of dollars on accountants and lawyers, if we cannot even get in the ballpark on price, terms, and conditions? Let's keep the horse in front of the cart. Let's cross this first bridge, or if not, move on to another business.

And remember that a lawyer's job and an accountant's job is to protect you—not to do the deal. They can never get in trouble for recommending "no"; they can only get in trouble for recommending "yes." Also be a little nervous about a lawyer who spends too much time "servicing" his clients. You might want him to work on a specific fee structure. (When I grew up in a small town surrounded by farms, we used to politely say that a bull was "servicing" a cow.)

One of the main reasons foreign buyers (new Americans) are buying so many businesses successfully is that they make an offer and negotiate. For instance, let's say I list a convenience store with an American seller and let's say that seller is asking $300,000, all cash, for the store. My good American-born buyer looks at the business and says, "Three hundred thousand dollars? That's too much," and he only has a $50,000 down payment anyway. Without negotiations, there is a no sale every time.

Now along comes a Korean-born new American. He looks at the store, and the seller tells him he is asking $300,000, all cash, for the store. The Korean gentleman only heard him say one thing: "I want to sell." He offers the seller $45,000 cash. The seller is outraged and says, "Absolutely not!" A week later he offers $82,000 cash, "Absolutely not!" A week later the undaunted buyer offers $82,000 cash and a small note back to the seller.

Three weeks later you go by the store and the Korean gentleman is now the new owner. You know why? He made an offer—and I'll bet you he didn't pay $300,000, all cash, for the store. He figured, "You want to sell, I want to buy—let's dance." We can learn a lot from new Americans.

16

Financing, Down Payment, and Terms

ONCE YOU LOCATE the business that you want and develop a "gut feeling" that tells you this business would work for you, the question is: can you agree with the seller on terms and conditions that you can afford and that are acceptable to him or her? The seller always wants more, and you always want to pay less, but there's an acceptable middle ground somewhere in between.

The Down Payment

The down payment is the most critical part of negotiations. Business brokerage is a "down payment driven" business. If we can work out an agreeable down payment, the rest of the terms and conditions can be anything that both parties agree to.

Now, we as Americans are not big savers. We make $100,000 per year, we spend $110,000. We make $200,000, we spend $210,000. However, that all changes when we make $300,000; at $300,000 per year we become Republicans and Republicans can always save money. The rest of us do not have a lot saved up, so when that income from the job stops, whatever it is—that's what we have available for a down payment and to live on.

How much total down payment ability do you have? A lot more than you may think. In addition to savings or cash in the bank, you have personal assets, stocks, bonds, retirement accounts [401(k)], automobiles, and/or real estate that can be liquidated and/or borrowed against to provide additional cash for a down payment.

Still other sources of funds are family and friends, who are what I call the "true venture capitalists" of small business. Looking for money from a "regular" venture capitalist for small business nowadays is almost as big a waste of time as it is for big business. I always tell my trainees, "If you ever find a venture capitalist, grab him, lock him in a closet, and call me. I'll be on the next plane. I've always wanted to see one of them." I've been hearing about venture capitalists ever since I got into this business over 20 years ago, but I have never actually seen one.

In small business, the venture capitalists are your family or friends. Your parents, in-laws, brothers and sisters, aunts and uncles, people who care about you, trust in you, believe in you, and will help you. I know that you never wanted to borrow money from your in-laws, but they just might be a great source of funds. Of course, they never liked you very much, but since their daughter married you, they'll help you out.

A word of business caution. This is a business deal, and it should be treated as a business deal. If you want to keep your family and friends, draw up a written note with agreed-upon terms and treat this obligation the same way you do any other. Besides, from the lender's standpoint, they want to help you and they want you to succeed, and if they can earn a little interest on the side, why not?

A 401(k) account may be liquidated if necessary or, under some unique circumstances, Sunbelt can show you how some of the money may be used for the purchase of the business without liquidating the 401(k). Now I know at first you say, "Oh no, that's my retirement, my nursing home money, and I have to pay a penalty to cash that in," or, "I'm saving that money for a rainy day." So what? If you don't have a job, you are already retired and it's raining. How are you going to eat? It's your money; it may need to be invested in your new venture.

The main thing I always come back to is this: if you can put down however much in a down payment and perhaps make that amount back and possibly more each year for the rest of your life and hopefully have a valuable asset to sell when you do wish to retire, this puts the "risk" into proper perspective. And remember, you've probably already put out hundreds of résumés for a job and no one has called you back.

Your Home as an Asset

Another often-used personal asset is your home. You may have a home valued at considerably more than the existing mortgage, and you may be able to borrow the equity through an equity line of credit or a second mortgage that is secured by your home, or you may actually refinance your home.

However, though your home may be one of the best sources of funds, it is different from the other potential assets to turn into cash. Mainly because your house is where you live, and you do not ever want to lose your house. If you do, where are you going to live? In a tent? With your in-laws?

Should you decide to use your house as collateral for a home equity loan (provided your wife, who is absolutely petrified, will allow it), then that is okay by me. It is your asset, and I believe the equity you have built up is also your asset to be used however you see fit. However, don't ever "cross collateralize" your house. In other words, you can use your home to borrow the equity, but do not ever use your home as additional security with a seller.

Here's what I mean, and this is very important: Let's say that you borrow part or all of the $40,000 down payment in our example against your home as equity and you use that as your down payment. I have no problem with that. However, the assets of the business that you are buying should secure the $60,000 note back to the seller. Do not also secure that $60,000 business note by adding the additional security of your home, no matter how badly the seller, and particularly the seller's lawyer, wants you to. Just say, "My wife won't let me," because if she's smart, she's not going to let you. And remember, if she can't stop you, there is always Daddy.

Another important point is that if you're going to get an equity line of credit or second mortgage on your house, do it while you still have a job and do not tell the banker you are going to buy a business. Otherwise the banker will have to put on a "commercial lending" hat and look at the business's financials for debt repayment. This could mean no loan.

Creative Financing

Assuming one way or another we've put together almost enough of a down payment to satisfy the seller, we may still be a little short. If we are, we may be able to run inventory down a little after closing to pay a short-term note, or allow the seller to do that before the closing. Either way, it could provide another $10,000 to $15,000, depending on the business.

Another way to get the seller a bit more cash within the first year of the sale (usually we think in terms of one year relative to income) is by agreeing to pay a small balloon payment, or "catch-up" payment, after the business's busy season or after Christmas. You may be able to sell off some unneeded equipment or assign a portion of profits of a particular product or service as additional money to the seller for the year.

One way or another, through creative problem solving, you have to arrive at a total down payment that works for you and the seller. The terms and conditions on the note balance can be anything that works and is agreeable. You can do a straight monthly payment of principal and interest amortized at an interest rate over 5 years, 7 years, 10 years, or whatever number of years is agreeable to you. This is not determined by an interest rate, or "prime rate," set by the Federal Reserve; negotiations set it.

I have done deals at 6 percent interest with only interest payments for 24 months, then the note balance is amortized at 6 percent interest over 15 years with a balloon payment of the balance due after 7 years. I have also done deals where there is no interest. Simply take the balance due and divide it by the number of months over which the payment is due. For instance, a $60,000 balance paid over 60 months (5 years) is $1,000. Nobody says you can't do that.

Also, I have had situations where there is an agreeable deal between a buyer and a seller, but the business is headed into the slowest time of the year in terms of the cash flow. Let's say that we're closing the deal on December 12 with $40,000 down payment, and the balance due of $60,000 is payable over 60 months at 7 percent interest. The monthly payments would be $1,188.08, normally beginning 30 days after closing, January 12.

However, both buyer and seller realize that the slowest time of year for this business is January, February, and March. One way to make the deal more workable for the buyer, and therefore increase his chances of success—and at the same time increase the seller's chances of getting paid (lower risk for the buyer and the seller)—is to get both buyer and seller to agree to delay the start of the monthly payments for four to five months. Instead of beginning the payments on January 12, what if we started the payments on April 12?

Now with a bank, the first thing they would say is, "Hey, what about the interim interest?" What interim interest? If both seller and buyer agree, we'll start the same monthly payments as agreed, $1,188.08 per month for 60 months beginning April 12 instead of January 12. Nobody says that you can't do that. Everything is negotiable—everything.

Some folks would call that "thinking outside the box." In small business negotiations, *there is no box!* There are no sides, no top, no bottom, and no front or back. If there are agreeable terms and conditions to the seller and to the buyer, we have a deal.

And remember, if the deal works for the buyer, the buyer will be successful and the seller will get paid. That is exactly what they both want.

Seller Financing

I have mentioned several times that if a seller will not finance part of the purchase price, I won't buy it. That is absolutely true, and I tell all my buyers and sellers this fact. Sometimes, when I first list a business for sale, I have a seller tell me he will not finance the purchase price because he is sick, or he is retiring or getting a divorce or moving a thousand miles away.

The market doesn't care about that any more than the market cared that you invested most of your life savings in Lucent, Webvan, Enron, or WorldCom.

The baseball rules still apply. Most of my buyers still have only from $15,000 to $60,000 down payment ability, and the banks won't make small business acquisition loans. So, probably the only way for a seller to get the full market value of the business is to finance the difference between the down payment and the balance due, whether he wants to or not.

The ability to get bank financing for part of the purchase price gives the buyer a reassuring "second opinion" that he or she is purchasing a good business. That the bank or SBA agrees to lend part of the purchase price provides a comfort level that this is a business that can pay off the debt service and make you a living.

If he can, the business broker will often try to help you get third-party financing. You can get a bank loan on some businesses. However, the bank loan can also bring up some other problems. If a bank makes a loan (SBA guaranteed or not), it will want a "first position" security interest or mortgage on the business's assets. This means that the seller's mortgage or security interest, if any, will have to be behind the bank's security interest.

Often, the seller will say, "I don't want to be behind the bank," to which I'll have to respond by explaining another of the rules of nature, "The big dog don't eat last"—and the bank is always the big dog. That means, of course, that if the buyer is not successful, cannot pay the bank, and the bank forecloses, the only way for the seller to get the rest of his money is to take the business back and pay off the bank.

Also, remember that small business is a relationship business. When the seller lists the business, he may say, "I'm not going to finance anybody." Well, I wouldn't finance just "anybody" either. But what about lending these nice people some money once you have met them and developed a relationship with them? And after the marketplace has shown the seller that what I've told him is true: (1) most real buyers cannot cash them out, and most rich folks won't buy a business; and (2) the banks won't lend because of the seller's financials, not because of the buyer's credit. And especially after the buyer has offered to put down everything they've got in a down payment. Once you have a *personal* relationship, then we can work on building the *financial* relationship.

Now, in developing a financial relationship between the buyer and the seller, you have to remember that they both have their own perspectives. And out of their perspectives come their perceptions, and their perceptions are their realities. Here is an example (from an idea I got at an excellent seminar presented by Bob Davies, an outstanding motivational speaker and personal coach from California). Let's draw a curved line on the page like this:

If I were to ask the seller (point A) whether this is a convex line or a concave line, he would say, "This is a concave line."

"Are you sure?" I would say.

Yes, he's sure, and you know what? He's absolutely right. From the seller's perspective that is a concave line. The end points are pointing toward him.

Now I ask the buyer (point B), who incidentally is looking at the exact same line (but from a different perspective), "Mr. Buyer, is this is a concave line or a convex line?"

He would say, "I can see it perfectly and it's a convex line, the end points are pointing away from me."

Well, they are both absolutely right. They are looking at the exact same thing but never from the same perspective. And out of your perspective comes your perception, and your perception is your reality. "I like a big city." "I don't like a big city." "I like cold weather." "I don't like cold weather." "I think she is a pretty girl." "I don't like her." "I think he is doing a great job." "I think he is a bum." "I like the restaurant business." "I don't like the restaurant business." And so on.

Now let's apply perspective and perception to our financial example (from the previous chapter):

Selling price $100,000
Down payment   −$40,000
Note due to seller $60,000

From the seller's perspective, and particularly from his attorney's perspective, he'll say, "I'm very worried about this buyer. He's only putting down 40 percent. We have got to have some *additional* security to make sure we get paid." That sounds so very logical from the seller's perspective.

However, from the buyer's perspective (assuming he's only got around $40,000 total life savings that he can get together, beg, borrow, or steal), is this *only* a 40 percent down payment? Absolutely not! From the buyer's perspective this same $40,000 down payment is a *100 percent* down payment and commitment. It is a *total* commitment. It is all he's got to give.

So the seller and the seller's attorney insist that we need additional security. They are not going to take back "just" the business assets as security for the $60,000 note. They need additional security, such as the buyer's house.

That just sounds so logical from a seller's perspective, but this is what the buyer hears: "I'm not comfortable that this business I'm selling you is worth $60,000, so we need some additional security."

"What!" says the buyer. "If the seller doesn't think the business is worth $60,000, then why am I paying $100,000?"

That is a pretty good question, put in the proper perspective. Plus, when I tell the buyer he's got to also put his home up for security, I probably just killed the deal.

I do not blame the buyer. I would not put up my house to buy a business. It is just too much risk. In fact, if you look at what just happened, the "risk-reward" ratio got turned upside down on its head. What if the buyer got hit by a truck, or the highway department digs up the street in front of the business for five months for a new water line?

The buyer could lose his entire down payment (life savings). He could even lose the business back to the seller, and if he pledges his home, he could also lose his house—everything in one fell swoop. That is too much risk, and remember, we weren't dealing with a risk taker to begin with.

There are other ways to further protect the seller's security within the business:

1. Find the best buyer in the market by researching the broadest possible buyer base.
2. Make sure there is a good training and transition period for new management that makes for a seamless transition.
3. Make sure the terms and conditions of the sale allow the buyer to be able to "stand up under them" and be successful so he can pay his obligations to the seller and be able to make a living.

4. Require that a constant level of inventory be maintained at all times to ensure the value of the security. Require a monthly sales or financial report for as long as the seller has a balance due to allow the seller to be helpful if the business starts getting off track—before we have a train wreck.

5. Require that all FF&E come under the security and that any and all "after acquired" or replacement FF&E come under the security as well.

These things help the deal work for both buyer and seller; therefore, they increase the security for each and also lower the risk for each. The continued success of the business works for all parties.

17

The Right of Offset

The Teeth in Owner Financing

O NE OTHER VERY important part of a relationship between the seller and the buyer is the *Right of Offset*. This means the right of the buyer to put teeth in his reliance on the seller's warranties and representation about the business, including his verbal warranties and representation about the cash flow of the business.

For instance, every note we write in a Sunbelt transaction has written right across the face of the note from the buyer to the seller the following phrase:

THIS NOTE SUBJECT TO OFFSET

Now, that does not mean that the buyer can simply refuse to pay the note, because if he does, then the seller can foreclose and take the business back under the terms of the note and security agreement. However, there are two specific circumstances that allow offset.

The first circumstance is *material misrepresentation*, which is a legal term for fraud, and the second is *undisclosed liens* that impede the buyer's clear title to the business's assets that are not properly disclosed and/or addressed by the seller before or after the closing.

Material Misrepresentation

Let's look first at material misrepresentation. Say that the seller has represented to the broker and to the buyer that the business is doing $350,000 per year in annual gross sales and that he is making around $50,000 per year true owner net. That fits my 10 to 20 percent rule, so I am comfortable that the owner is probably telling the truth.

Now understand that this is the seller's representation, not the broker's. The broker does not warrant anything, just as the accountant doesn't warrant anything. Have you ever seen the front cover of a business's financial statement? The accountant has a disclaimer as big as a barn door, even if they have been doing the books for the business for several years. The disclaimer says (paraphrasing), "All of the information herein has been provided by the management" and "management has chosen not to comply with any of the rules of GAAP"—Generally Accepted Accounting Practices—"and therefore this accountant and this accounting firm makes no warranties and representation that this information is current, complete, or accurate."

If this business owner's accountant who does his books every year won't warrant the information, then certainly the business broker won't either. Nor should he. The only person who really knows the whole truth is the seller; therefore, he's the one who should warrant that the information is true and correct to the best of his knowledge. And the buyer certainly has the right to rely on the seller's warranties and representations.

A note of levity: I've always liked the H&R Block ad that proclaims, "If you're audited, we'll go with you." Of course they will—it's not their problem. Sitting in front of an IRS agent, when asked, "Where did we get this information?" they will simply say, "The business owner right here gave it to us."

Often, a buyer will want to meet with a seller's accountant. That's fair, but always keep in mind that what an accountant knows about a business is limited to what the seller tells him or turns over to him, no more, no less. This is important.

Unlike a lawyer, there is no client privilege with an accountant. In other words, if you were my lawyer, I could admit to you, "Yes, I killed that guy." My lawyer would say, "For goodness sake, don't tell anybody else that. We'll plead not guilty, and let me do all the talking from here on out." My lawyer, no matter how horrendous the crime, cannot *ever* be a witness against me or he would lose his legal license. That is called client privilege.

The accountant does not have that client privilege. If he were made aware of unreported cash or inappropriate allocation of resources or unreported inventory or sales, he would then become a coconspirator and could get into almost as much trouble as his client. He could lose his license. So most accountants have adopted Mr. Bill Clinton's "Don't ask, don't tell" policy to small business accounting. They don't ask you about any information, and you do not tell them anything other than what you turn in to them. Therefore, it always comes back to this fact: the only 100 percent reliable source of complete information about the business is the seller.

This reality has been blatantly exposed in the relationship between the Enron Corporation and its accounting firm, Arthur Andersen. We will all be witness to the accountant-client relationship as this debacle plays out in the court of law and the court of public opinion. However, these were audited financials, and small businesses seldom, if ever, have or need audited statements. Small businesses don't ever have reviewed statements; instead, they most often have compiled statements (sometimes referred to as "shoebox accounting"). That is why I keep referring to seller financing as the seller putting his money where his mouth is.

Now back to our example. The buyer has made his decision to buy, based on the warranties and representations of the seller. Again, the seller said that his gross annual sales were $350,000 and he was personally making $50,000.

The buyer buys the business and takes over the management. He says to one of his key employees: "Mary, I understand that you did $350,000 in sales last year." Then Mary's jaw drops and she says, "Who told you that? Man, last year was really slow. I'd be surprised if we did half that in annual sales." Wow! We've got a problem.

Now here are two scenarios to make my point. In the first scenario, let's assume my example of a $100,000 purchase price with $40,000 being the down payment and $60,000 on the note back to the seller. Good for you!

You go to your lawyer, after you get your head out of the toilet, of course, and tell him what happened, and the lawyer says, "Give me $15,000 and we will sue the bastards." Lawyers always seem to want $15,000. Sue them? You may not even be able to find them. If you are dealing with a crook, then you are dealing with a crook. But in this worst-case scenario you cannot find the seller and cannot get your down payment back. Thus, you may have just purchased the business for $40,000 *total*. Certainly you are not going to pay the balance due on the note. You will offset it because of material misrepresentation.

In a second scenario, let's say that the buyer was able to pay all cash, $100,000, at closing. He got the money from family and friends or the bank, and of course the seller would always rather have cash.

You close and take over the business and say to one of your employees, "Mary, I understand you did about $350,000 in sales last year?" Mary's jaw drops, etc.!

Guess what? You just bought it. Even if you do want to sue the seller, what if you can't even find him? He's gone, and the lawyer still wants $15,000. That is why I like owner financing.

So, how do you know if the seller is telling you the truth about the business? How do you know that the cash flow is there; that there is not a significant environmental problem lurking that could put you out of business? How do you know that there isn't major competition or an industry change forthcoming that could put you out of business? How do you know that the equipment isn't ready to break down or that the employees won't walk out or that the main customers won't pull their business once you buy it and take over?

The best way to arrive at a comfort level and a level playing field is that the person who knows the answers to every one of those questions better than anyone is willing to invest in your success. And incidentally, in the first scenario above, where the seller is lending you part of the purchase price, these problems almost never come up. If the seller is materially misrepresenting the business or hiding something that could be a major problem, he won't lend you the money to buy it. Remember that we are not normally dealing with a foolish seller.

Undisclosed Liens

The second right of offset is provided to protect the buyer in an "asset sale" from undetected or undisclosed liens.

Here is where the sale of a business differs significantly from the sale of real estate. In real estate, if you have a debt instrument, it has to be in writing. That's the law. And it has to be recorded in the county where the property is located. That is the law. That is the reason why, when the bank makes you a loan to buy real estate, it requires that your lawyer (he's not really your lawyer, he's the bank's lawyer, but his or her fees are in the closing costs, so who cares) give the bank a title opinion and provide the bank with a title insurance policy on its first mortgage position.

The lawyer can do that in a real estate deal; he simply goes down to the courthouse and checks the records. You put down 10 percent, the bank lends you 90 percent, and there is 100 percent of the purchase price right there on the table. The lawyer pays off any and all liens, records the new mortgage, and certifies the title.

There is not a lawyer in Pennsylvania, Texas, South Carolina, Florida, or Tennessee who would *dare* give you or anyone else (including the bank) a title insurance policy on a business. Wouldn't touch it with a 10-foot pole. It doesn't exist. Cannot get it.

In business, we are dealing with chattel mortgages, UCC-I (Uniform Commercial Code) rules, and there is no law that says if a legitimate business debt is not in writing or that if it is not recorded at the county courthouse then it's not a valid debt or lien. Plus, there may be other potential lienable circumstances against the assets of the business that are not on any record. These could include accounts payable, withholding or other tax problems that have not yet surfaced, and lawsuits (business and personal) that have not yet been filed, or recorded, but are on their way. All of these examples could come up and bite you afterward because when the closing attorney or escrow agent searches the business title, they won't show up.

In the scenario with $40,000 down payment and $60,000 due on a note to the seller—again, good for you. You have $60,000 to offset any undiscovered liens that impede the title. In the second scenario, with $100,000 cash up front at closing, you run the risk of having something show up that would impede or cloud your title. Too bad, you just bought it.

The positives of owner financing just make good common sense. This is the best way to build a solid foundation from which to take the "leap of faith" necessary to buy a business. Are there still some risks? Of course, but seller financing allows you to go as far as you can to lower or mitigate the risk, to help you keep a level playing field and get you to your goal line! And remember, when you get to your goal line and you buy a business, the seller just successfully got to his or her goal line and sold a business.

In a transaction where you can get an SBA or bank loan, the seller is signing warranties and representation to the U. S. government that all the information is true and correct—so your "teeth" is an SBA loan.

Always work with your attorney to arrive at a level playing field that both protects you and sets up a workable framework for success. An experienced business attorney adds great value to the transaction.

Some Words of Advice

E VERYBODY THINKS ABOUT the future. Some folks even worry about the future. Where will we be in one month, six months, two years, or twenty years? Who knows? Certainly I don't, and neither do you. We will never know what life has in store for us. But we have to do the best we can to plot and plan.

One of my favorite moments in one of my favorite movies, *Out of Africa*, is when Meryl Streep's character recalls that Robert Redford's character had always said, "One of the reasons that the Lord made the earth round was so that we couldn't see too far down the road." There may be some truth to that. You never know for sure what lies down the road. You just have to trust in God or fate, or whatever you prefer, and prepare as best you can for today and for tomorrow.

A good friend, Jed Waterbury, once told me, "If you want to hear God laugh out loud, tell Him that you have a five-year plan." (You have to think about that one for a while.) Now that doesn't mean you don't need to plan and prepare for the future. Only a foolish person would do that, and you are obviously not a foolish person. You are reading this book! (You may have to think about that one for a while also.) However, usually the most reliable source of information about the future is the past. What will happen is best described by what has happened and what is happening now.

When John Naisbitt wrote his runaway bestseller, *Megatrends*, the most interesting thing about all of his research was that it was a collection of facts about what was already going on. The future trends were a continuation of things that were already happening. It was just that most folks didn't see the trends because they were too busy with the present and trying to look into the future.

Using the *Megatrends* method of looking into the world of business and of work, we can best project the future based on our recent past and what is happening now.

I do not foresee a time when big business will start rehiring folks by the tens of thousands or when job security will return to the point where you will stay with one company through retirement. I only see continued "rightsizing" as companies stay lean or get leaner, as continual improvements in technology and robotics eliminate the need for workers, and as foreign competition eliminates or replaces the jobs in the United States.

Now that's not all bad. There is a great deal of good in those realities. You just have to make the necessary course corrections in your thinking and perceptions and perhaps take that leap of faith and go into business for yourself, and thus provide for your own income and job security.

Americans are a fiercely independent and self-reliant people. We always adjust and adapt to the challenges we face. These next few years will offer great opportunities to small businesses that address a market need and provide a product and/or service that the market wants, needs, and will pay for.

As a man or a woman, and as a provider, it is up to you to make the living for your family, and I believe with all my heart that owning your own business, or your own "farm," will help you do exactly that. And I also believe with all my heart that normally an existing business or a franchise with a proven track record of success is safer than a start-up for all of the reasons we have talked about. Even big businesses normally see the advantages of merging and acquiring (M&A) rather than starting from scratch.

The main thing, as Nike says, is to JUST DO IT! Find the business that works for you. Look at the amazing opportunities that await you in your new world of work. Do your research on the marketplace and on yourself and get going. Focus and prepare and pray and you will find that a lot of folks will help you. We all like winners. We like folks who take their talents and multiply them.

Now as I said in Chapter 1, I don't know much about life and business except what I have learned from the last 61 years of my own life and from the other lives that I've studied, particularly as related to business. And as I have said throughout, when it comes to small business, your life and your business are one and the same. What you do that affects your personal life also affects your business life, and what you do in your business life affects your personal life and therefore your family.

There have always been and will continue to be ups and downs in business and in life. Try to learn something from both and make good course corrections. When you think you are right, listen to your feelings and don't ever, ever, ever give up. Henry Ford is credited with the saying, "If you think you can do something, or if you think you cannot do something; you are probably right."

Here is a simple poem that I keep on my desk:

Press On

Nothing in the world can take the place of persistence.
Talent will not; nothing is more common than unsuc-
cessful men with talent.
Genius will not; unrewarded genius is almost a proverb.
Education alone will not; the world is full of educated
derelicts.
Persistence and determination alone are omnipotent.

—AUTHOR UNKNOWN

So, although most of us have been given the tools, talents, and the time, we have to provide the "sweat equity," or the work. We have to do our part to make our family farm or family business work. Long hours, hard work, more hard work, and tough decisions are always worth the effort because your future will be provided for.

A good investment in yourself is to read books, listen to tapes/CDs, and learn from the experience of others. One of the best business books ever written, in my opinion, is Napoleon Hill's classic *Think and Grow Rich,* which was written in 1937. Two themes that drive his philosophy of business are (1) "of the twelve things that constitute real riches in a man's life, money is number 12," and (2) the basis of most all successful business is found in the "Master Mind" theory of linking other people's brains together with your own in a spirit of harmony to achieve a common goal. This works in business as it does in families, government, charities, and other organizations.

As my partners, associates, franchisees, and I have had the pleasure of growing Sunbelt, we have learned a lot about ourselves, about surviving in business and about businesses all across America. We've learned firsthand how difficult, exhausting, challenging, frustrating, and exciting growing a business can be—we lost money for the first nine years. There is never enough time, never enough money, and good ideas (even great ideas) don't always work. Never give up, but try to honestly recognize when a course correction is due.

When we first started growing Sunbelt, my wife, Elaine, and Dennis's wife, Nancy, worked with us for several years, most often for no pay. Later, Dennis's youngest son, Dennis, came to work with us to develop our technology department and later our Web site. In the November 2001 issue of *INC* magazine, Sunbelt's Web site won a first place position in the annual "Best Web Sites in America" contest out of 800 business entries. Sunbelt has also been rated number one in business brokerage almost every year since 1995 by *Entrepreneur* magazine's annual ranking of the "Top 500 Franchises in America." Technology has contributed greatly to our success. Thomas Moore is now head of technology at Sunbelt, and he does a great job.

We later hired Dennis's older son David, a CPA with the Marriott Corporation, as our vice president and CFO, and my nephew Ben Pendarvis, who I rely on and trust as my assistant, and later one of my sons-in-law, Jason Martin, to run our call center. Jason had seven years experience in running call centers for banks and other big businesses.

This brings up another very important point. Make sure that the family member/employee is a justifiable employee, not just a make-work family member. At Sunbelt we strongly believe in family business, and it has worked well for us. We enjoy it. Plus, sometimes your family will work for less than anyone else when you are just starting up!

Keep Your Costs Down

Keep your expenses down, since there is never enough money. Try to do what Dr. Thomas Stanley and Dr. William Danko suggested in the book *The Millionaire Next Door*. Live *below* your means. Order the house wine. It's just as good, and in 10 minutes it won't matter anyway, except that you'll have more money left. Use a debit card instead of a credit card, and you won't be spending money that you don't have yet.

Another thing is to always, always watch your overhead. I like to think that I'm frugal, but most other folks think I am cheap. Either way, I'm pretty good at squeezing a nickel. Here are a few business tips on keeping costs down:

- Never buy a new car. A slightly used car with a little warranty left is a much better value, and after a week it's a used car anyway.
- Don't spend so much when you have it, so that you will have something when you need it. Eat out with your spouse at good but moderately priced restaurants. Have a "date night" every week. It's important.
- Never pay to fly first class. The back of the plane gets there just as fast, and you never have heard of a plane "backing" into a mountain, have you?
- Stay at moderately priced hotels and motels. They usually offer a clean room and a free, healthy breakfast. (FREE— America's favorite word!)

If I have to pay over \$70 per night at a motel, I feel as if I need to stay up all night watching TV and running the hot water, trying to get my money's worth. If you're by yourself and you drive, you can sleep a while in your car (while not driving!) on a two-day road trip, then check in after 6 a.m. in the morning and stay through that night for one day's room rent rather than two (take two showers, though). Don't tell anyone else you did that, but you just saved \$70.

The one advantage that I got out of my Citadel education and U.S. Army Ranger School Training is the ability to sleep anywhere, anytime. That is especially helpful when you are flying at night, or overnight on the "red-eye" back to Charleston from the West Coast. Also, if you're coming back from a trip and you're by yourself and you've got to leave on a very early flight in the morning, why not catch a ride with a friend to the airport the night before, sleep at the airport, and save the \$70 room fee and \$25 cab ride? Folks look at you a little askance, but by early morning you get in line with everyone else and you have just saved \$95. (And you might even write a book while you are spending the night at the airport.)

Here's another tip: don't ever borrow money if you don't absolutely have to. It's not that I don't like to borrow money—it's paying the money back that is so difficult and unpleasant. If you don't pay folks back, they'll get difficult and unpleasant. Another thing: if your true owner net is 10 to 20 percent, debt at 8 percent interest or more, or factoring your receivables, can eat up all of your profits, and then you're working for the banks or the moneylenders rather than your family. If you do borrow money, pay it back as soon as possible.

Find a Business You Like

Always try to find a business *you like*. Now it's still going to be work, it's not play, but I believe that if you can ever line up what you like to do with what makes you money, then you have hit a home run.

When we opened a Sunbelt office in Minneapolis/St. Paul in 2000 with a good friend, Scott Evert, we went out to supper in downtown St. Paul after the first day of training. You may or may not know this, but the creator of Peanuts (the Snoopy and Charlie Brown comic strip), Charles Schulz, was from St. Paul, and he had recently passed away. Several statues of Snoopy decorated the downtown St. Paul area as a tribute to one of the city's favorite sons.

Now, I am not the brightest person in the world, but I have always been a pretty good "reverse thinker." It seems to me that sometimes I see things differently from some other folks. I think that I must have run into a lot of trees or fence posts when I was a kid. Here's what I imagine about Mr. Schulz.

I imagine him as a young man going home and telling his father, "Daddy, I think I am going to drop out of school. I have this great idea about drawing a comic strip about a dog. What do you think?" His dad probably would have said, "Are you crazy? You have to get that education and a good job with a good company like 3M or something."

Thank goodness he did what he wanted to do and liked to do, and he enriched the world with his wonderful talent and stories. It is still on the first page of the "funnies" section as Classic Peanuts.

When we opened our pioneer office in Los Angeles in 1995, with our very successful franchisees Ron and Vickie Hottes, I had another thought—about when Mr. Walt Disney first had to talk to a banker about his crazy idea. I can just picture it: Walt walks into the banker's office all excited and says, "Mr. Banker, I've got a great idea. I am going to open up a family recreation park based on a theme of a little mouse named Mickey and his girlfriend Minnie. What do you think?"

I am sure the banker listened to him somewhat amusedly and said, "Eh, we'll get back to you on that one, Walt, but thanks for coming by." Now if he was lucky, the banker gave him a ballpoint pen with the bank's logo on it and a token to get out of the parking lot. Fortunately, he persisted and persevered and did what he liked to do, and he changed the world.

Just remember that whether you're working for yourself or for someone else, you are always working for yourself. You are always self-employed.

Also remember that all business value comes from sales. I heard this from Brian Tracy, a wonderful businessman and inspirational speaker: Dun & Bradstreet have done several surveys on what makes businesses successful and what makes businesses fail. You know what the single biggest reason for business failure in America is? *Low sales!* You know what the single biggest reason for business success is? *High sales!* Everything else is commentary!

Jack Welch, the very successful and now retired CEO of General Electric wrote a book in which he said many things I agree with, but I would like to share two points in particular with you.

First, he said that if you were going to manage a business successfully in today's world, you have to constantly change the business to keep up with the constant changes in technology and in the marketplace or these changes will pass you by.

When I was growing up, G.E. made refrigerators, stoves, and lightbulbs. Now they are one of the largest financial businesses in the world; that's where they make their money. They probably now "job out" or contract out the stoves, refrigerators, and lightbulbs.

The second thing he said that I absolutely believe is that if you are going to manage a business successfully in today's world, you have to deal with the world *as it is*, not as you would like it to be. Now, is that good advice or what? He is a very smart man, and many folks consider him one of the best CEOs ever; however, his prenuptial agreement ran out too soon. Who in the world would have thought a 25-year prenup would not be long enough?

Why don't small businesses keep better financial records? Why don't the banks make small business acquisition loans? Why don't colleges and universities teach classes on the "real world" of small business management? Why aren't there any $100,000 per year salary positions with job security in my town? Why don't stocks always go up? And why don't I have more specific information and direction in order to make a better decision?

I don't know the answer to these questions, but I do know this: They just *don't*. I cannot change the world, but I do hope that I can help some folks navigate the real world of small business and how to deal with it a little more realistically. Especially when it comes to your understanding of the real value of small business—*to you*. And most things that apply to life generally apply to business.

On a More Personal Note . . .

I have seen debt break a lot of good businesses and good folks even though they worked hard and smart, myself included. In fact, one of the reasons I've always stuck with St. Phillip's Episcopal Church in Charleston, besides it being a beautiful place to worship and the mother church of the Episcopal diocese in South Carolina, is that during the mid-1980s they were about the only folks in Charleston that would take my check. Incidentally, in 1729 a daughter of Joseph Pendarvis was married at St. Phillip's, and approximately 300 years later my daughters were married there. I love weddings—like education (more on this below), they are a wonderful investment in your children.

And speaking of investments: always try to get up by 6 a.m. to watch the sunrise, and start your day off with private time and prayer or your meditation of choice. Be thankful for the wonderful blessings in your life. This simple act is a major investment in the man or woman in the mirror.

I always begin my training sessions with a short prayer, and I ask my trainees to join me, if they wish. I figure if you can pray before a football game, you sure ought to pray about some of the most important decisions that you are going to make. Such as, how you are going to provide a living for your family. Now, other folks may not need prayer, but I sure do.

As for your general health and welfare, I will confine my recommendations to: eat right, exercise moderately, get a reasonable amount of sleep (but not too much), don't smoke, love your children and grandchildren (they are your greatest gifts), and try to make at least one woman or man happy; or at least one of them at a time.

If you were fortunate enough to be born in America, realize that we owe a lot of brave folks a lot for our freedom and opportunities and responsibilities. If you weren't born in America, get here as quickly as you can and you will be warmly welcomed as a new American. There is no other place on earth like it, and we are truly, truly blessed and living in the land of opportunity.

Use your learned and inherent talents to the best of your ability, and make sure that you do not let your education get in the way of good old common sense. As Will Rogers said: "Common sense is not as common as most folks think." He also said, "I never met a man I didn't like." What a great statement—obviously, ol' Will never met a few of the folks you and I have met over the years.

But education, both formal and informal, is important. Invest in the best education possible for yourself and your children. My sister Lois and brother-in-law Tommy Harper have four children that they raised with a lot of love, direction, encouragement, and high expectations. Their oldest son, Tom, graduated from Duke University and Duke Law School; son number two, Mikell, graduated from West Point in 1995; daughter Abney graduated from the University of North Carolina and law school at Tulane; and son number three, James, graduated from West Point in 2002. That is a strong focus on education, and it will pay off in their children's success. My sister-in-law, Debra Bowen, is a smart computer programmer who put herself through college the hard way—at night. She graduated with honors, from the College of Charleston, with a degree in physics, whatever that is. Her extra efforts in education have paid off.

At the moment, we at Sunbelt are working with the Business Department at The Citadel to add a "leg" to entrepreneurial education. Normally, this discipline focuses on doing a business plan and start-ups, but with the leadership of the dean of the School of Business, Colonel Earl Walker, Ph.D., as well as Colonel Mark Bebensee, Ph.D., and Major Wesley Jones, Ph.D., we are adding "Buying and Building" a business. Instead of big business Mergers and Acquisitions, we will teach the business principles of "Acquire and Grow"

Also, remember that most big businesses started off as
all businesses. Hopefully you will enjoy this journey
ard success. Even enjoy traveling, as I do, if your market
s you there. But, with luck, your favorite place in the
will be your hometown and your own backyard. You
ight surprise yourself and even your father-in-law. By
y, he actually likes you more than you might think
you are good to his daughter and you are the father
andchildren. And grandchildren are *the BEST!*

appropriate to small business. Also, speaking of principles,
The Citadel leads the way in teaching "Principled Based Leadership" in business. Good for them!

I believe you should always give God back His 10 percent
in whatever manner you feel is right, and give it happily.
Based on my experience, a 90 percent true owner net to you
and 10 percent to your partner is a great deal for you. Occasionally, you probably ought to give some of your 90 percent
to the government too. All in all, they spend it well, and of
course in the United States, the government is "us."

And when things do not go as you hoped and planned,
try to make the best of your circumstances. For instance,
when I ran for public office and lost, here is a little poem I
used to help the "healing" process:

Make Friends

> *The poll is over*
> *The results are known*
> *The will of the people*
> *Has been clearly shown*
> *Let's forget our differences*
> *Let bitters pass*
> *I'll hug your elephant*
> *If you will kiss my ass!*

—Author Unknown

By trying to remain friends with all parties and never
burning bridges, we can have the opportunity to serve and
help in ways we do not expect. In 1992 some of the folks who
were not for me in politics asked me to serve as chairman of

the People for Parks committee to champion the passing of a $34 million bond referendum to improve the Charleston County park system. To show you how good my timing is, two weeks after I agreed to serve, they announced the closing of the Charleston Naval Base, our largest employer.

However, in spite of the projections of gloom and doom economically, we got 61 percent of the vote for parks, even though every other bond referendum lost that election year. We can sell what we believe in, and investing in yourself always makes sense.

Final Words

I will leave you with this simple philosophy: Try as best as you can to add value to every relationship and every situation that you find yourself in. Never burn bridges with relationships, especially those that affect your family members. If you ever get upset with someone, especially a family member, sit down and write them a letter, explain and express your feelings completely, but never mail it. Try to see the other person's point of view. Don't ever expect anyone to do something that he or she doesn't think is in his or her best interest. Then you won't be disappointed in them.

Never miss an opportunity to attend a wedding, a funeral, a child's play or game, or to visit a friend who is ill. I know that you might be very busy, but always make time for family gatherings or these opportunities will pass you by (and you may need to borrow some money at some point). You will never regret the time spent with these activities in life, as they are the *most* important.

Then, do what you say you're going to do, if possible, and treat every person with respect; learn from folks who disagree

with you even though they may be a pain i
already know what folks who agree with
know how much you appreciate them,
ily, friends, and husband or wife.

Try your best to adhere to sched
you set them out. It is good to cha
however, remember, "only Robin
his work done by Friday."

Take your business and yo
don't take yourself too seriou
to the words of wisdom a
favorite poets and singer
"Changes in Latitudes, Cl
couldn't laugh, we just
Went to Paris" he sir
motion, if he likes y
magic and some of
way." Visit Marg:
adise," but in Re
Enjoy your life
the hard times
Be a happy

Be frier
long he'll
agent or

Be
bless
just
m

The Future of Sunbelt

WELL, TO SHOW YOU how life mirrors art—guess what? We have recently sold my "baby," Sunbelt Business Brokers. However, I sold it to the only folks that I wanted to—the Sunbelt franchisees, my friends and partners.

Over the years, especially as Sunbelt grew to a strong market position in our industry, several people and companies have been kind enough to express an interest in buying Sunbelt. I told them, "Thank you for your interest; however, Sunbelt is not for sale. It is my life's work."

When my friends and franchisees, Carl Grimes of Fayetteville, Arkansas, and Dan Elliot of Houston, Texas, first approached me at the IBBA conference in New Orleans about selling Sunbelt, my reply was the same: "Sunbelt is not for sale, this is my life's work." Well, Carl Grimes said, "Ed, Sunbelt is my life's work also. We share the same goals and visions, and we want Sunbelt to continue to grow and succeed."

As Carl, Dan, and I talked, I realized that this just might be an answer to a prayer. Sunbelt had gotten too big for me to run by myself, and Dennis, my partner, was focusing on other business. Dan said, "Ed, you were running the company like a small private business, and it needs to be run like the big business it has become for us all to reach our potential."

He was right—this last year Sunbelt did over $1 billion in transactions and generated over $78 million in commissions.

I agreed to sell Sunbelt with three provisions: (1) that the possibility of ownership would be offered to all Sunbelt office owners, (2) that I have an opportunity to buy back as much stock as anyone could own, and (3) that I have the opportunity to help run the company for the next five years. They agreed.

So Dennis and I put a price on Sunbelt that we considered fair, and unfortunately someone had taught the steering committee how to negotiate a business deal and we ended up with an offer somewhere in between the asking price and the original offer. Then the due diligence committee came in and told me I had some warts. To which I said, "Warts? You think my warts are bad, you ought to see my abscessed tooth and hemorrhoids." Anyhow, we ended up with further negotiations and a fair deal where the sellers were getting less than they thought the business was worth and the buyers were paying more than they would like, but a deal was accepted by all sides (with a lot of owner financing).

I believe the Lord sends you the right people at the right time. Bill Davoli is a Citadel graduate, and he had recently joined our Charleston Sunbelt office. He has built a small business from scratch into a big business and sold it to a bigger company, then managed the big company's sale in a "rollup" to a public company. His help in the Sunbelt sale to the Sunbelt Acquisition Company (SAC) was invaluable. Bill understands small business and large business, and he served as the liaison between SAC, Dennis Sr., Dennis Jr., and myself. He justifiably had the trust and confidence of all parties (and believe me, there were a lot of parties to this transaction). The deal began closing around 10 a.m. on Tuesday, December 10,

2002, and we finished at the lawyer's office at 10:30 p.m. The attorneys did a great job, and *we did it*!

Our new founding board of directors (Carl Grimes, Dan Elliot, Deb Moore, Dan Pedersen, Steve Rosen, Ron Hottes, Scott Evert, Bill Davoli, and myself) had its first meeting and we came up with three major objectives:

1. Focus on helping our Sunbelt offices to be more successful
2. Focus on helping our Sunbelt offices to be more successful
3. Focus on helping our Sunbelt offices to be more successful

The new management team of Ed Pendarvis, president, and Bill Davoli, COO, started immediately to formulate and execute plans as approved by the board. I sent out an e-mail to all Sunbelt office owners following the closing, and here is an excerpt:

> Let me just end this letter by thanking each of you for your support, trust, and assistance. Elaine and I feel that our business relationship and your friendship mean more to us than you will ever know. Building this company has been a labor of pure bliss as I have gotten to know each of you personally and all of your brokers over the years.
>
> With your continued help and the Lord's continued help, we will be able to have a major positive impact on thousands of folks' lives as we help them sell or buy a business when it is the right time in their lives to do so. You are the experts, you are the knowledgeable

brokers who know how to help solve problems and get the deals done. I am proud of all of you.

Over the last year, we have added Seminar Education to our programs, and in March and September of each year we hold more than 200 seminars all across the United States and overseas. They are FREE seminars about the "Secrets of Buying, Selling, and Valuing a Business" promoted jointly by Sunbelt and this author, local Chambers of Commerce, Small Business Development centers, and local colleges and universities. More educated buyers and sellers can make better decisions on behalf of themselves and their families.

At Sunbelt, we also have put together an owner financed note guarantee program and mezzanine financing for owner financed businesses, as well as SBA financing. If the owner will finance part of the purchase price, which shows that he or she has confidence in the continued success of the business, then we also are able to feel confident about the business's continued success.

At the Sunbelt 2004 annual meeting, our twenty-fifth anniversary of Sunbelt, we had the "entrepreneur's entrepreneur," Peter Shea, the CEO and owner of Entrepreneur Media, as our keynote speaker. Peter's life in business is a classic example of a risk taker. He started his work life as an undercover narcotics officer in San Francisco, or as a "bullet catcher" as he calls it, and then rode the ups and downs of real estate development through the 1980s. Then he bought and significantly developed a franchise company, Stained Glass Overlay, into a worldwide company with over 350 franchisees. When he visited *Entrepreneur* magazine because they were doing a story on his company, he decided to buy the magazine company and grow it. He has done just that, and his company has probably done more to promote the true entrepreneurial spirit than any other company or organization. We applaud his success in helping others.

Looking to the future of Sunbelt, I believe that we have just begun. As the United States and, indeed, the world move back more and more to small business as a "best solution" to provide for your income and job security, Sunbelt will be on the cutting edge of that re-migration. Our franchisee-owned network, with the board's continued leadership and the Lord's continued help, can truly help a lot of folks get to their goal line.

We hope you are one of them!

Best wishes and respect,
Ed Pendarvis, CBI

Acknowledgments

At Sunbelt we've been fortunate enough to attract some wonderful and bright franchisees (partners) and associates to help us develop our market presence. I have learned a great deal from each of our franchisees, especially Tim Rogers in Sacramento, California; Dan Elliot in Houston, Texas; Ron Hottes in Los Angeles, California; Carl Grimes in Fayetteville and Ray Gorcyca in Little Rock, Arkansas; Bill Tschudy in Raleigh and Bill Law in Charlotte, North Carolina; Scott Evert in Minneapolis, Minnesota; Steve Thomson in Irvine, California; Doug Jackson in Washington, D.C.; Debbie Moore in Reading and Dave Ball in Pittsburgh, Pennsylvania; Dan Pedersen in Kansas City, Missouri; Kipp Krukowski in Cleveland and Bill Eaves in Columbus, Ohio; Pat Lawrence in Portland, Oregon; Michael Drury in Salt Lake City, Utah; Doug Walker in Chicago, Illinois; "Tex" Garner in Fort Worth and Laurel Johnson in Austin, Texas; Ray Boreham in Atlanta, Georgia; Majid Zarinbaksh in Bethesda, Maryland; Franco Ferrari in Orlando and Mike Richards in Tampa, Florida; Jeff Moody in Dothan, Alabama; Brian Mazar in Louisville, Kentucky; Charlie Broadwater in Richmond, Virginia; Mel Eisen in Danbury, Connecticut; Herb Lonegrass in New Orleans and Bob Bourgeois in Baton Rouge, Louisiana; Gilles

Maillart in Gainesville and Bud Diem in Sarasota, Florida; Steve Stone in Virginia Beach and Nancy Winters in Fairfax, Virginia; Sonny Adams in Memphis, Tennessee; David Bayne in Omaha, Nebraska; Steve Rosen and Ron Hoxter in Philadelphia, Pennsylvania; Bonaventure Wakam in Ventura and Joan Young in San Jose, California; Brian Cross in Denver, Colorado; Roger Hutson and Matt Ashburn in Des Moines, Iowa; Tom Miller in Mesa and Bob Bohacik in Tucson, Arizona; Satish Patel in Boston, Massachusetts; Steve Goldberg and Jack Armstrong in New Jersey; David Yezbak in Columbia, South Carolina; Len Krick in Las Vegas, Nevada; Kelly DeWitt in Dallas, Texas; Greg Kells in Ottawa, Canada; Greg Lange in Thailand; Stuart Montgomery in the United Kingdom; and Robert Dandt and Lawrence Wong in Hong Kong, China.

And every Sunbelt broker past, present, and future and their wives and husbands; and Michael Auten, our CEO from Atlanta. You are the reason for our success, and Elaine and I thank you for all you do.

Index

About the Author

Ed Pendarvis is chairman, president, and founder of Sunbelt Business Brokers Network, LLC, the largest small business brokerage network in the world with 350-plus offices in the United States and 11 foreign countries. He is a 1965 graduate of The Citadel and served two years active duty in the U.S. Army Artillery. Ed served as director of The American Legion Palmetto Boys State Program for 11 years and as chairman of the South Carolina Department of Youth Service Board (Juvenile Correction and Aftercare) for 6 years. He received the state's highest civilian award, The Order of the Palmetto, in 1978 by the Honorable James B. Edwards, Governor (R), and received The Order of the Palmetto in 1983 by the Honorable Richard W. Riley, Governor (D). Ed has been a real estate broker since 1970 and started in business brokerage in 1982.

He serves as a member of the Better Business Bureau Board, The Palmetto Boys State Committee, the Board of the International Business Brokers Association (IBBA), and the Advisory Board for The Citadel, School of Business Administration.

Ed is married to the former Elaine Bowen of Charleston, South Carolina, and has five beautiful daughters and four wonderful grandchildren—"and grandchildren are the best." He is a member of the St. Phillip's Episcopal Church in Charleston.